# SSSHHHH… ..I.T HAPPENS!

## (I.T's life Jim but not as we know it)

# By

# Paul Hookham

ISBN: 978-1-4717-3832-6

# Dedication

I would like to dedicate this book to everybody who has worked for or with I.T organisations. I.T's never a dull life!

I certainly appreciate all of your efforts; for your dedication to causes - especially lost ones; for your never ending ability to make me laugh out loud or leave me totally exasperated; for your bloody-minded determination to never say Yes or No to absolutely any question. Take a bow!

It would also be remiss of me not to thank my employers. Your generosity and blind optimism over the last four decades, has enabled me to see the world on expenses.

Finally, on a personal note, I'd like to thank everybody who has contributed to this book, either directly via reviews or indirectly, by being the inspiration behind some of the stories. I simply couldn't have done it without you.


May you all live well and prosper.

# About the author

Paul Hookham is one of those I.T people who always turn up to the show with extensive war wounds resulting from far too many valiant attempts over the years at delivering projects, on both a permanent and mercenary basis. He has worked for many blue-chip organisations in software project management, software development and application support as well as infrastructure development and support. His talent knows many limits.

Paul has experience of most hardware platforms as well as a wide range of lifecycles and methods. He is an advocate of quality and believes passionately in customer delivery and only working on activities that the customer considers valuable.

Even after a career in technology that has spanned almost 40 years he remains, and will always remain, one of the bewildered.

Contact paul@exceedus.co.uk

# FOREWORD

## Welcome to the world of the good and the true

For some reason that totally escapes me and without wishing to insult the literary world, some bright spark once said that everyone has a book inside them. So armed with this unpleasant and somewhat pain-inducing thought, there now follows my humble attempt to prove or disprove that particular theory.

I have read hundreds of books as, throughout a long career, my work has fuelled much travel. Well to be completely honest with you, a lot of time has been spent hanging around airport lounges and railway stations waiting to be called for much travel. Thinking about it, a more accurate description would be not only waiting to be called for much travel but also having to find out for myself the latest excuses for the absence of much travel.

This irritation has become 'de rigueur' as the owners of the airport lounges that I use have, in their infinite wisdom, kindly removed all departure screens and stopped all flight departure announcements from the front desk.

On the up side, the nicely colour co-ordinated airport lounge staff consistently deliver these highly unpalatable messages to customers with style, a smile, a hint of panache and facially, looking a shade over-orange! 'You need to keep your eye on the screens just outside of the lounge, so you don't miss your flight, sir' is a well-practiced line always delivered in a smooth, subtle and sometimes mesmeric fashion. On the down side, the railway companies tell you nothing of use – ever!

Even my somewhat cynical response of 'So what am I paying for exactly?' is met with a sympathetic look usually reserved for children who have grazed their knees in the playground at school.

It does, to some extent, defeat the object of buying a pass to the lounge. I thought to myself why on earth would a service company treat their customers like this?

This is a common theme throughout the book – delighting customers and only providing services that are of value to them. What value did I get from the removal of all information from the airport lounges?

I must apologise profusely as I have, as usual, digressed, and probably lost most of you already. I have agonised about the content. What should I write about? Who'd want to read it? Then, in a flash of inspiration, I thought of all those people hanging around airport lounges and railway stations waiting to be called for much travel. The prime audience, I hope, are all those I.T folks who fly around the world so frequently that they almost single-handedly keep the airline industry afloat or to be more politically correct, up in the air.

I also recalled that aforementioned bright spark recommended that a subject be chosen that one knows in detail. So, a risky approach has been taken and I have written about my profession and the people who work in it. I will address the issues they've raised, some of the quite preposterous things they've said and done, the subsequent barrels of laughter they've induced and the incredible amount of work they've produced, whether it be valuable or wasted.

**Early Health Warning**: At this stage I must point out that this book contains very little in the way of technical content. It is a story of people, their behaviour and how they are managed. It is not for the faint hearted or software engineers.

So if you view Information Technology as a dull profession inhabited by people who can remember exactly how many ants they trod on when they were at school, well so did I when I joined it kicking and screaming in 1972. There are certainly some I.T. disciplines where this viewpoint stands up in court. It is, however, light years away as a generalisation.

I can say without a shadow of a doubt that every single day has been different, bringing with it new challenges and unconquered mountains to climb, usually but not always as a result of ill-informed commitments made on our behalf by people who really should know better. Senior management are certainly paid a considerable amount more money than us to know better, aren't they?

So armed with my alphabet of Frequently Asked Questions, some of which are even relevant to the subject matter, I will attempt to enlighten you all based on four decades at the coalface. I will admit to you now that I may well have fabricated a few questions and answers but, protected by the aegis of poetic licence, I have sourced the majority from various communication channels both inside and outside of the workplace. These channels are often referred to as canteens, coffee bars or pubs.

Some of my answers may even be construed by many as somewhat facetious or even cynical. There is more than an element of truth in this as it is my quest to entertain as well as enlighten. However, I promise that everything I have written is honest, genuine and pragmatic. It is, I hope, also entertaining and usually, but not always, as a direct result of my learning experiences, or mistakes as we used to call them in the 1970s.

I really hope you have as much fun reading the book as I've had writing it. It really has been a labour of love and has taken far too long to complete.

Now before we get started I will warn you now that unlike a lot of business books I've read, I will buck a worrying trend and won't give you any guidance at all on how it should be read and in what order, as you may confuse me with someone who cares. I will, however, tell you that as the subjects are in alphabetical order it is highly unlikely and completely coincidental if there is any continuity whatsoever. So feel free to read any of it, at any time, in any order, as this is my excuse for consistent repetition on a handful of what I consider to be critical issues to be addressed. If you ask me nicely I may even tell you what they are.

Now that you have made an excellent procurement decision and are staggering back to your seat in the lounge with news of the latest delay, please rest assured that the proceeds of your purchase will go to a very good cause. That I will happily guarantee.

Thank you all very much and enjoy the show.

June 2012

*'A positive __Attitude__ may not solve all your problems, but it will annoy enough people to make it worth the effort' – Herm Albright*

**ARE APPRAISALS A TOTAL WASTE OF TIME?**

**Q:** Our I.T. department has just completed its annual round of staff appraisals and various strata of senior management have reviewed the performance of all of their people against their objectives, assigned a performance rating and agreed any subsequent salary adjustments.

Senior Management then spent 3 days at a 5-star hotel in Disney World making sure everybody was rated fairly using a very confusing and somewhat suspect moderation process. They also used the time to do some peer ranking as well. Do you think this was the best use of the company's time and money, especially in today's economic climate?

**A:** To be frank, it really depends on how good your senior management team are at agreeing objectives, making sure everybody understands them, how they will add value to their customers and how people are to be measured consistently against them. There also needs to be a process for regularly updating objectives when the latest must-do initiative transforms by osmosis into this week's top priority. No doubt you have your own personal views. Mine are not very positive although I have very occasionally been pleasantly surprised by a couple of companies who actually perform these appraisals very well. These are a rare breed sadly!

So, without wishing to sit on the fence, I strongly believe that appraisals in isolation are a complete and utter waste of time and money that add little value to either individual performance or customer service. I have found the process quite useful though when trying to exit poor performers, purely on the basis of using all the pretty forms, produced at great expense by the army of HR consultants on display.

1

Maybe I should turn the question back on you. Can I ask whether you think your department's performance has improved as a direct result of doing appraisals? Are things getting done better than before? Is the delivery culture improving? Is your customer happier than before? If not then you have the answer to your question.

Oh and by the way, if the senior management team went all the way to Florida and didn't go on theme park rides such as Space Mountain, Splash Mountain, Soaring, Test Track or Big Thunder Mountain, then it certainly was a total waste of time and money. Forget the peer ranking and buy everyone Disney tickets. People might end up having some fun, getting some teamwork going and taking a much improved espirit-de-corps back to the workplace.

## ANALYSIS MISUNDERSTANDING

**Q:** I have heard it said that analysis is a total waste of time. Given that a substantial amount of any project's budget is spent on requirements gathering and it's absolutely critical that the requirements are clearly understood, don't you think this was a very unprofessional thing to have said?

**A:** If I had said that then yes, it would have been, without qualifying my view. Let's assume for the purpose of this exercise that this is exactly what I said. Well, a lot of time is wasted in analysis, irrespective of the first 4 letters in the word itself. Weeks and often months are spent documenting requirements in a format that encourages each stakeholder to interpret them differently – and then everyone expects them to be complete and a perfect design delivered as a result. How so?

Why won't we accept the obvious that until the customer can actually touch and feel the solution, then the requirements remain volatile, incomplete and subject to change? Why won't more organisations take a good look at what the real value of requirements gathering is and the best way to approach it?

If things are really going to change, then let's start the design and build as soon as possible and then any changes will materialise much quicker than if the build had been delayed until all the requirements had been signed off in user blood. Chunk the requirements into small increments and get the customer to prioritise them based on those that will deliver the highest value – and then deliver them as quickly as possible.

What I have also learnt is that what really annoys customers is when different people from the same I.T. department keep asking them the same questions over and over again, every time a new project launches. For goodness sake, if you are going to spend light years documenting requirements, at least have the sense to follow a process so that they can be used again in the future. Don't start with a blank piece of paper every time! Maybe even more radical, don't even start things off as a project!

## ASSESSMENTS – CAN YOU HANDLE THE TRUTH?

**Q:** Our CEO was convinced that he had a world-class software delivery capability in his organisation and recently returned from a conference where the subject of benchmarking was fairly high on the agenda. I have absolutely no idea on what basis he arrived at his 'world-class' conclusion, as we have no data whatsoever to back it up with. It also doesn't feel very world-class round here.

He certainly had no clue as to why so many so-called high maturity organisations are from outside the UK, and given this scepticism he immediately authorised a full blown, no holds barred, tell it like it is, nuts on the line, tackle out assessment using the CMMI® appraisal method, which I believe is known as a SCAMPI 'A'.

The outcome of the assessment was a maturity level of 1. If it's of any help to you, we apparently used the staged representation of the model as the consultants told him that he would get a plaque on the wall with this approach. What does Level 1 mean and why did it result in our I.T. Director being summarily dismissed? Is there something fishy in the SCAMPI?

**A:** I can't begin to tell you how much is wrong with that question? I don't really know where to start, but I feel certain that my response will not be brief. First and foremost, your CEO is completely deluded and I recommend that you avoid him, even with the comfort of a ten-foot barge pole and asbestos gloves. I can only imagine that he has been somewhat boastful within his immediate circle of influence or peer group and his ego has been badly bruised by the appraisal outcome.

He has done exactly what a number of soccer club chairmen do. He has expressed full confidence in his I.T. Director and after one bad result, booted him out as well as blaming everything from the trick questions in the appraisal to the state of the washrooms. Certainly no sign of a positive spin such as 'the result was disappointing but we now have the roadmap we need to move forward'.

Secondly, Level 1 generally means that working practices are ad-hoc. Ad-hoc is a Latin phrase that means for this purpose. In terms of the results it usually means that there may be some evidence of good work but it is not pervasive throughout the projects that were reviewed, and the interviews probably identified that good practice is usually ditched when the going gets tough.

Ad-hoc assessment results usually occur when the credibility of the I.T. organisation is placed squarely, and in my view negligently, on the shoulders of a few Clark Kents and Captain Fantastics in the company who play the hero and save the I.T. Director's reputation at the eleventh hour on EVERY SINGLE PROJECT.

No practical experience ever gets documented, nothing is repeatable and no learning ever occurs and will never occur because these superhumans are always rewarded at appraisal time and openly praised by senior management. In other words, this is the way the company wants its I.T. function to operate. Message delivered and received loud and clear.

Let's return for a moment to the appraisal result. I always interpret ad-hoc as a polite term used in this instance to preclude the use of a more derogatory term i.e. crap! Please don't be offended by this as crap is pretty common and has a very broad church ranging from mud-sucking crap to fairly sophisticated crap. It will all become clear as the appraisal results are played back to you by the lead appraiser.

If your CEO has any sense, a dangerous assumption perhaps given his actions to date, he or she will sponsor an initiative to act upon the findings and get something done to improve things for both your customers and your people, especially customers. An action plan based on the findings would be good with the focus on activities that are prioritised to deliver the earliest measurable benefits to all stakeholders.

But whatever you do, you must avoid gathering together a group of waifs and strays, that no-one else knows what to do with, to write a forest of Victorian-novel processes and then expect anyone at all to have the slightest interest in them, let alone use them. Fix the things that will make the biggest difference to your customers and use credible practitioners to lead the charge. They will have been champing at the bit anyway, but have been put off historically by the culture of command and control or something similar.

Sadly, your I.T. Director was just a rabbit in the headlights, being in the wrong place at the wrong time and unfortunately, like the rabbit, collected the number plate and left the building. That I'm afraid is both corporate life and the ball game.

Finally, to answer the last part of your question, I do not believe there is anything fishy in the appraisal. These are always conducted by people who have been formally authorised, via an intensive, tough and expensive route. You should get a professional, detailed and consistent result irrespective of who conducts the appraisal for you.

However, the law of averages says that some appraisers are either more or less lenient than others but this is human nature and the responsibility of others to resolve if it ever becomes a problem in the industry. The results from each of the practices under review are binary. You either perform an activity or you don't. You cannot be slightly pregnant in the appraisal world.

Remember though, adherence to a model is not a guarantee of either better performance or happier customers. Many high maturity organisations are not as effective as they should be and a different way of working is almost certainly needed to complement the newly improved practices.

# ANNOYING ACRONYMS

**Q:** Every time I attend one of those cryogenically induced, I.T-led death by slide-show sessions, not only am I losing the will to live but I'm also furious about the continual use of acronyms that nobody understands but you I.T. guys. Even the last Q &A used the acronym SCAMPI without explaining what it stood for. Can you (a) stop it immediately and (b) explain the most commonly used acronyms so that at least I have a snowball's chance in hell of understanding what on earth you people are talking about?

**A:** OMG, sorry, Oh My Goodness! You are of course coming from the totally deluded view that we want our customers to have the first clue what we are talking about! How do you expect us to retain our mystique and justify our enormous costs if people like you start to understand what the hell we're doing? However, in order to placate you, I have risen to the challenge and have listed here a few of our favourite acronyms. There are a few curved balls to annoy you even more but probably not much more than you are already.

I can't explain what they mean or in what context they can be used as I'd get lynched by my colleagues in the Magic I.T. Circle.

1.  **SCAMPI** – Standard CMMI Appraisal Method for Process Improvement.   Happy now? Any the wiser? Glad you asked? Difficult to bring it into any conversation whatsoever, isn't it?
2.  **GIGO** – Garbage In Garbage Out - self-explanatory but explains why later stages of testing, for example, often fail to meet their objectives and take forever.
3.  **KISS** – Keep It Simple Stupid! It's not rocket science. Well unless it's NASA (OMG - another acronym – sorry!)
4.  **DCSOS** – Different Company Same Old Stuff - the grass is not always greener on the other side, but the stuff smells the same and not a very nice odour either.
5.  **NUMP** - No Ugly Men Please - nothing to do with I.T. but nonetheless very funny in lonely-hearts columns.  Are you getting really cross yet?
6.  **JFDI** – Just eFfectively Do It! – an I.T. Director's much-quoted phrase always expressed with feeling, passion and a soupcon of a threat.

7. **JFDIP** – Just eFfectively Do It Please – the word please has been added for companies who desire to be employers of choice and who really care about their people!

8. **FPA** – Function Point Analysis - don't ask – just don't bloody ask OK!

9. **KULOC** – Thousands (**K**) of Uncommented Lines Of Code - often used by people as a size measure of defect density or productivity. These people don't know the difference between New York and New Year – so ignore them!

10. **WIIFM** – Not a World War Radio station but what's in it for me?

I hope you feel much better now and I trust that these examples have helped to illuminate you or maybe it's made things worse. Have a nice life or **HANL** as we call it in I.T. circles! Finally, one observation if I may from your question. Can I just ask what the acronym Q&A stands for? OK - That's it – I'm off...........

# B

*'**Bureaucracy** defends the status quo long past the time when the quo has lost its status' – Laurence J Peter*

## I.T'S A BUG'S LIFE

**Q:** Every time I receive a new release of software, I spend an unacceptable amount of time finding and reporting bugs to my suppliers. What's the problem? Why so many and shouldn't they be fixed for free?

**A:** Cracking question. Yes of course they should and if all was fair in love and war then they would be. The trouble is that the world we live in is not quite as black and white or as simple as that. If the software you acquired was commercially produced then the likelihood is that you would get your issues fixed for free; maybe not tomorrow, or next week, or next month but you'd get them fixed depending on what it stipulates in your contract. More often than not they will be fixed in the next scheduled product release. If they were causing absolute havoc with your customers then you will almost certainly be given a temporary workaround. If you don't then make a fuss and if all else fails refuse to pay the suppliers' expenses. That should do the trick.

On the other hand, if the issues arise from software developed by your own internal I.T. organisation then you have to pay for their salaries and benefits so it can't be for free. Internal organisations are cost centres and not profit centres and there's the rub. A number of companies that I've worked with seem quite happy to accept having say, 500 I.T. people, split equally between Development of new functionality and Support for fix-on-fail and in some cases small enhancements.

Now just think about that for a second. In this example, that's 250 people supporting a live product that's already been through all of its review and

9

testing cycles. This could easily cost six figures a day to feed, which if scaled up for a year, could reach eight without even breaking sweat.

What's going on here? How much more new functionality could be delivered if support didn't have to be funded at this level? Ok this is an extreme example but it does highlight a potential nightmare, especially when economic conditions are tough.

Most customers of I.T. projects assume fault fixing is an acceptable cost of the software business and until they wake up and smell the coffee and challenge these inflated support costs then nothing much will change. Remember – the customers have already paid for quality or at least assume they have!

To use a much used building analogy, you wouldn't consider spending a hefty sum having an extension built on the back of your house and then spend the same amount every single year thereafter simply to stop it falling over, would you? So why is this accepted in the I.T. world. Stamp your feet, make some noise, throw your teddy out of the pram and insist upon better quality. If you don't whinge, then keep writing those support cheques year on year, directly from your profit and loss account - ouch!

Before I close this one, we need to agree that these are defects we are talking about here and not bugs. Bugs are nuisances that fly in and infect things and are entirely outside of your control, so there's nothing you can do about them. Defects do not fall into this category at all as they have been injected into the systems, maybe over many years, by the developers, designers, testers, implementers and even customers who have at some stage worked on the systems. Defects are very much within someone's control to fix and it takes strong management and team pressure to ensure they are not tolerated and it needs impacted customers to make their displeasure known if they are not happy.

So are defects avoidable? Of course they are if continuously improving and fit for purpose quality practices are used by the teams and always performed on every project. Unfortunately, reviews rarely get planned into the schedule by project managers unless they live in a high maturity world and even if they are planned in at the start of the project, many organisations remove them from the schedule as soon as the pressure to deliver reaches fever pitch.

Then what happens? All of a sudden a critical process such as product reviews gets canned and a 'we'll find the defects in test' strategy takes over. Not surprisingly, some defects are found but many more slip through the net into a production system and those who find them throughout the lifetime of the system are people like you, the customer.

I read a book some time ago and it defined the quality problem superbly. The author offered the view that 'using test as the only means to find defects is like trying to lose weight by weighing yourself more often'. Basically if you want to deliver quality then you need to do effective reviews of the work products and get the defects out, the earlier the better. Oh and if you want to lose weight then eat less.

I hope this answers your question. I simply don't understand why more customers like you, aren't demanding better quality products. A challenging question to ask your suppliers is what they would do differently if your continued custom was based entirely on the number of defects found by your people. I am certain you would get a totally different approach then.

# THE SCOURGE OF BUREAUCRACY

**Q:** In the 1980's we were promised the paperless office, reduced red tape, more automation and less hassle all round allowing us to concentrate on our jobs. Is it me or have things got worse instead of better? What's the problem as it's doing my head in?

**A:** In my humble opinion the problem is caused by the 'It's more than my job's worth' mindset and a refusal to relinquish the comfort blanket of form filling and outdated ways of working.

We have many square pegs in many round holes. These functions create overhead costs and become solutions looking for problems. They do not, in any way, shape or form add any value to anything really. It gets worse as their authority, influence and budgetary power often outweigh what it should based on their contribution. These people are never empowered to say 'Approved' - but can say 'No' at will. Ridiculous!

My view is that if they are not directly contributing to the delivery of value to all stakeholders then they ought to go and do something else. Perhaps the penalty is to have some of them fill in all the forms they have designed until they become a gibbering wreck like you.

These additional costs inflate the amount that I.T. charges its customers and it makes us prohibitively expensive. So if you are in one of these support groups then please treat I.T. as a customer. I appreciate that it's only exceptional management that will address this but in the meantime it's good to get things off one's chest occasionally. Do I sound bitter?

## THE BUSINESS CONTRIBUTION

**Q:** Do you think that I.T's business customers understand what their roles are?

**A:** Short and sweet. Some do, many don't. It all starts off nicely. A senior executive has a brilliant idea. It then gets a bit of flesh on it, maybe with some conceptual thinking and this culminates in a business case. Ultimately some form of external commitment will be made if the case stacks up, sometimes with input from I.T, sometimes not. The outcome is often something commonly known as a project with ballpark costs and timescales. What could be simpler?

The trouble then starts as middle or lower management try and squeeze in more and more functionality for the same price or lower, based on the same end date or sooner. Gold plating of requirements often occurs and before you can say 'Less is good', the senior executive's idea is lost in the ensuing fog and the business case is annihilated before anything is built. Sadly nobody realises and when they do, only a few care. It takes guts to can a project when the numbers don't add up any more.

I'm going to digress a little from your question but I think it's a good time to do so. Lack of I.T. engagement up-front isn't necessarily a problem by the way although it's always nice to get involved early to help shape the solution. It also gives executives some assurance that the project or programme is operationally doable before they make any 'go back and prepare for government' presentations to their board or heaven forbid, their market. The fact remains though that whether I.T. likes it or not, it is a service to the business that generates the income to pay its salaries so it needs to support the hand that feeds it.

It may well be that the only thing that is fixed is the end date so teamwork between customer and supplier is critical. If I.T. engages in the way it should and doesn't throw a hissy fit because it hasn't been consulted on everything then it will become an asset as opposed to a liability. Too many I.T. functions are targets and to be honest, deserve to be unless there is an absolutely rigorous focus on customer delivery.

So to revert to your question, the more the critical activities can be shared, the greater the chance of success. As far as the business roles are concerned, they will be responsible for any changes to business process that the automated solution demands. They will take care of internal and external communications, coming up with the business requirements hopefully in short iterations, ensuring the business case stacks up and continues to deliver value as time elapses and money is spent. They will also provide the project sponsor, chair project boards or steering groups and of course, ensure effective User Acceptance of the solution, including any business related training.

These are the primary business roles. They are challenging to perform but not that difficult to understand. Where the problems lie is when they start playing I.T. expert and have a view on how things should be developed and how long they should take, based on nothing more than a whim, the desire to look good to their management and of course, they used to work in I.T, didn't they?

If you are sponsoring a project for the first time, please ensure that you come prepared to all meetings and ensure you make your people available to support the I.T. guys as they need it. It is not a good use of people's time to turn up at steering groups to simply find out what's going on. Please review the latest progress reports or other papers beforehand. Ensure you are fully briefed as even though your time is precious, people need their issues resolved quickly. Time spent at meetings coming up to speed is a total waste of everyone's time and no-one wins.

Don't play Father Christmas when it comes to handing out requirements. Be minimalist and only authorise what's absolutely necessary and valuable. The I.T. industry does not have any real track record of delivering large, functionally complex projects, so if you can preclude gold-plating, phase the implementation of the requirements based on value and importance then the chances of success increase by an order of magnitude. It really is not a game to see how many features you can squeeze in. You are setting up I.T. and ultimately yourself, to fail.

Finally, business people need to keep to their commitments. If you slip a day or two in your piece of the action, don't think it doesn't matter and then expect the I.T. piece to claw back the time you have lost for them. They can't, so take some of the responsibility yourselves and share your concerns so that a good outcome can be achieved. These are your projects not I.T.'s so please behave like they are.

I have toned this answer down quite considerably, believe it or not and would like to apologise to the many fantastic customers out there who work brilliantly with their I.T. counterparts. Where have you been all my life?

## BEWARE OF THE BENCHMARK

**Q:** Have you any experience of external benchmarking of I.T. costs and capabilities and what are the pros and cons?

**A:** Yes I have thanks and not all of it is good. However, as long as everybody understands why it's being done and what will happen with the results then it can, on very rare occasions, be a very positive and illuminating experience.

Negativity creeps in if people simply collect data and aren't told why they are collecting it or how the results will be used – this is asking for trouble. Street corner meetings will fuel rumours of outsourcing or headcount reductions and morale will plummet overnight, undermining any previous good work in this area. The seeds of fear and blame will be sown.

To have a chance of delivering a successful outcome for your company, I would recommend you consider some of the following: -

✓ Document your benchmarking requirements and select your suppliers diligently by getting a proposal from more than one specialist company - if you can find more than one that is.
✓ Communicate the rationale behind the benchmarking exercise to everybody and let everyone know what will be done with the results.
✓ Ensure your supplier is readily available, on-site if necessary, to provide advice, guidance and clarification throughout the data collection exercise. Some of the pro-forma they will have dished out may well be either out-of-date or irrelevant, so ensure immediate support is on tap to keep the momentum going and maintain credibility in the exercise.
✓ When you get them, understand what the results are telling you. Please bear in mind that a large proportion of the outcomes may have been influenced by people who no longer work for your company. This needs to be factored into your thinking when analysing the results and agreeing subsequent actions.
✓ Understand what is meant by a successful outcome. Don't just look at the cost per resource. You could have a reasonably expensive resource pool but it may be worth it if it's delivering double the output and quality of your benchmarked peer group of companies.

✓ Finally, prepare some sort of action plan based on the recommendations. It will have cost a significant amount of scarce budget to produce these, so treat the report as an asset and not something to gather dust in the bowels of your organisation. Seek resources from every level to get involved in resolving the major issues found and then most suspicions should disappear and something will get done.

# C

*'I feel that if a person has problems **Communicating,** the very least he can do is shut up'* – Tom Lehrer

## THE COMMUNICATION BREAKDOWN

**Q:** Although there has been an upward trend in most areas since our last staff survey, our overall communication scores have regressed by 20%. We have spent loads of time and money on communication-related activities including meet the boss lunches, posters and intranet newsletters. How come our numbers have dropped off so steeply?

**A:** I really do sympathise with you, just not that much. You can't please everyone with the poisoned communications chalice but you should be pleasing a lot more people than you appear to be. There could be a number of reasons for this. Apathy could be a contributing factor, although the apathetic will neither agree nor disagree with you as they are too busy removing large splinters caused by too much time sitting on the fence.

It could also be that you are: -

(a) Trying to do too much or
(b) Haven't asked everybody who does not attend the forums how they would like to be communicated to or
(c) Simply haven't accepted the fact that a critical mass are not in the slightest bit interested in any form of communication and certainly would not complain if you simply put it all on the company intranet where they can take it or leave it or
(d) All or a combination of the above.

As a general observation based on most organisations that I have worked with, there is nowhere near enough time given to the most effective communication channel of all – face-to-face.

Other contributing factors could be the number of people you are trying to catch in your communications net, what the subject matter is and whether you are targeting all roles and areas of interest.

In small organisations, you can easily set aside an hour a week to cover off most things at one session, with everyone present. This concept has worked well for me in the past. I have led a weekly session where everybody would come along for tea and cakes and ask whatever they wanted to. I would make any important company announcements as well as do my level best to answer any questions. Others were also invited to give an update on what they were working on. I take no credit for the format as it was already in place when I joined this particular company, but it was good fun and it worked for most people although you simply can't please everyone. At the very least I succeeded in force-feeding them with cake if nothing else!

In larger organisations this is not practical so consider setting up a group of credible volunteers to share the workload and deliver the messages in a timely fashion. Set up small groups and get them together at the same time each week so all the news is synchronised. Then if all else fails, stick your chin out, appoint a Communications Manager and then pray for a miracle!

## THE CONSULTANCY HERD

**Q:** As a long-term shareholder in my company I have severe reservations about the number of external consultants working in my organisation who seem to have found the solution to human cloning. Why do we need so many? What value do they add? Surely it must impact the bottom line significantly with questionable value and unclear outcomes?

**A:** I'd like to say that consultants are very clever people who fill knowledge gaps in organisations by the transfer of their wisdom and capability that will ensure that, when they all clear off, the victim organisation is managed more efficiently than ever before, thus providing better, cheaper and faster delivery to its customers. Sorry, this paragraph is long in both words and irony.

Just think of the majority of consultants as $21^{st}$ century Julius Caesars – we came, we saw, we invoiced! I would have written Veni, Vidi but I can't find a suitable Latin translation for invoiced. Input, as always, is most welcome.

In defence of our Roman invaders, it is a massive generalisation of course and completely unfounded. I have met some extremely sharp, bright consultants during my career; no please don't laugh, it's true. They generally fall into the Account Director or Pre-Sales Consultants category. They certainly won't be the ones you'll be getting! For some reason, senior executives get a warm feeling, just hold that thought for a second, when their projects and programmes of work are populated with the perceived best of breed or thundering herd or whatever macho Top Gun analogy is in favour at the time.

Sadly all you can do is grin and bear it and try to do as professional a job as you can in these extreme and difficult circumstances. One day though there will be another disaster and they'll get kicked out. You will then have a big smile on your face for about 10 minutes until you realise you're the one left holding the pup and have to sort out their mess and quickly.

Remember that many consultants don't get on by doing outstanding work for their customers. They get on by being good at consulting and doing outstanding work for their consultancy in terms of revenue generation.

Just thought I'd share these ramblings with you!

20

## COACHES NOT ALLOWED

**Q:** At my last interview I was delighted to hear that coaches play a big part in the personal development strategy of my new organisation. They aren't available yet but the company has aggressive plans to introduce them. Well I'm 6 months in and still waiting. Have you any insight as to why this might be and am I barking up the wrong tree? I am Swedish and we take our personal development very seriously. Our companies have experienced dramatic improvements in performance as a direct result of coaching. What's going on?

**A:** Having previously worked in a Scandinavian company, it was a real pleasure to see how they looked after their people and coaching featured heavily in this. It's terrific if your organisation has the right culture and is ready to invest significant time and money to make it work.

Sadly, I remain unconvinced that many UK companies welcome the concept of coaching as the rewarded behaviour usually centres on heroics so there wouldn't be much time for it as the people are too busy putting out big fires and chasing their schedules. There is also a deep layer of cynicism and inertia to be overcome in traditional hierarchical organisations.

Like you, I've seen the word 'coaching' used very frequently and it is in many project and programme manager job advertisements but I've only ever seen it offered once in my entire career. How sad is that? We must really care about the development of our people!

In my sparse experience of the coaching world, it works well if it is -

    A.  Offered as an optional service to employees.

    B.  Operated at a peer level i.e. hierarchy-free.

    C.  Performed by trained and motivated people.

    D.  Never used in any way shape or form to influence the outcome of employee appraisals.

    E.  A challenging experience for both the coach and the coached. It should never resemble a cosy fireside chat and at the end of each session, it should feel like it would after a strenuous workout at the gym.

    F.  Never automatically assumed that because you are a manager that it in any way, shape or form qualifies you to be a coach, let alone a good one.

G.  Not confused with mentoring. This is a totally different competence. Managers must be able to mentor or they should go and sell ice cream.

Coaching worked brilliantly for me so please feel free to try this at home.

# THE CULTURE CLUB

**Q:** Last year we appointed a new I.T. Director who immediately launched a Cultural Change programme. Before you could say 'Where's my office?' a Change Council was established, populated by a dozen people selected from various levels of the organisation. The Council reported directly to the I.T. Director for this particular piece of work. However, despite all of the focus and funding, not one thing has changed! Why is this?

**A:** If I had a pound for every time someone asked me that question I would have £2. No seriously, I'd be able to retire a wealthy man. Something has changed though. You are far more disgruntled than you were before the change programme kicked off. OK it's not the way things should have panned out but at least it's a change, albeit for the worse.

That gets the positives out of the way early which is always a good thing to do on the old motivational swingometer. I'm now going to ask you a handful of questions and if the answer to any of them is 'No', then you will understand instinctively why nothing has changed!

1. When you started, was it absolutely crystal clear where you were as an organisation, where you wanted to get to, why you wanted to get there and how you were going to bridge the gap between the current and target model. How would you know when you got there? I realise that is more than one question but hey, it's my book!

2. Did you really believe that these 12 disciples in the Change Council were capable of moving the culture of your entire organisation in the right direction, even with massive executive sponsorship? Did they have credibility, gravitas, influence and outstanding communication skills and by that I mean really deep listening and not just talking? Or were they the Dirty Dozen that nobody knows what to do with? In other words an influential manager has said 'Here's an idea, let's put the DD on the most important thing we're doing!'

3. Did you really have effective hands-on executive sponsorship and had it been sustained since the initiative started? By the way, I include all of the I.T. Director's management team in this and not just friends, socialisers and hangers-on.

4. Did anyone else in the organisation, particularly your key stakeholders, have the first clue what was going on and what was in it for them?

5. Did anybody in the organisation outside of the inner circle, show any interest or ask any pertinent questions regarding this change initiative?

So – did you answer No to all of these, some of these or none of these? If the answer is none then you've probably arrived in a good place but don't quite know it yet, but well done you, albeit still a tad worrying as you should have noticed an order of magnitude shift in performance! If the answer is all or some, then you have your reasons for the abject misery you are currently experiencing.

I've been in a similar situation myself so I do have a lot of empathy for once. In a previous job I held, when the thorny old cultural change issue was debated at an infamous executive management meeting, the following was heard from the boardroom. 'Why don't we change something; I don't care what it is, but change something – anything!'

As a result of that particular outburst, anyone working after 7pm didn't have to sign-out at security when they left the building. I think you'll agree that was a fantastic outcome for 12-person years of effort. The defence rests your honour.

# D

*'What I love most about **Deadlines** is the whooshing sound they make as they go by' – Douglas Adams*

## DANCING WITH THE DEVIL, GOING WITH THE FLOW

**Q:** I don't know if you remember me but we met at the first or second European Software Engineering Process Group conference in Amsterdam in 1996 or 1997. There was an after conference event at which you presented a piece about energising the workforce and the need for them to take on new ways of working that would deliver the sort of price/performance improvements that today's business demand.

If I remember correctly your story used a dance hall analogy and I remember being very impressed at the time but don't have total recall about why I was so enthused. Can you refresh my memory? My name is Alan Blast by the way (no – not really). Do you remember our conversation?

**A:** Well how could I possibly forget? After our little soiree you have always been known to me as A. Blast from the past (no – not really). The dance hall analogy changes between the working day, where I am the consummate professional evidenced by huge bouts of sage nodding and blah-blah-blahing and the evening, when I'm usually agonising over whether a fruity red or an oaky little white will get the job done. But, as your question is of a somewhat serious nature, I will attempt to refresh your memory with the family-friendly version.

For argument's sake, let's assume there are five numbers to be used when rating the performance of your people. This breaks them down into the following pigeon holes and enables us to see the wood from the trees. This revolutionary scoring system uses 1-5, the lowest being 1 and these are categorised as follows: -

**1** – These are your worst performers. You must get rid of them and quickly as they are dragging your organisation down to their level of incompetence and apathy at a phenomenal rate, annihilating morale and any hope of improvement.

**2** – These are the people that, when you ask them to do something, always have 30 minutes to tell you why they haven't got 15 minutes to spare. They're not the worst performers in the organisation but they are very, very close to being.

I used to dread that little tap on the door just before end of play on a Friday afternoon. I may have had a dinner engagement but hey, work is work, so you invite them in. A little bit of free advice at this point from bitter experience, never ever ask them any questions at all during this late slot or your backside won't wake up until Saturday lunchtime. Keep listening by all means but a question tends to spark a very long diatribe.

They will happily spend an hour in my office making me extremely late, undoubtedly incurring the wrath of the real senior management at home, and at the end of it they tell me that they didn't think I could help them much anyway. I end up covered in number 2. It's all over what's left of my hair, on my clothes, foaming around my lips and coming out of my nose. Hopefully you get my analogous drift.

**3** – These are very solid people and normally the vast majority. You can trust them with your last penny to do a good job for you but they will rarely go that extra mile. You know they are more than capable but they either lack confidence or interest. Don't annoy these people as without them you are up a gum tree without a flip-flop or similar mixed metaphor. They are the backbone of your organisation but just sometimes you'd like to use the verbal equivalent of a cattle prod on them to galvanise them into doing inspirational and challenging work.

**4** – These are the star performers. Without wishing to cast aspersions on any peer ranking exercises, in my experience a 4 is a 4; always has been and always will be. There are of course exceptions but there is generally another reason, certainly nothing to do with challenging work. If I had to pick a dream team of 12 people I'd have six 3's and eight 4's on the basis that I'm bound to get behind for a bit so I might as well start two over budget. This is for the benefit of those who immediately thought 'The man's an idiot, he can't add up'. Now you know that I'm just an idiot.

There would be no place in the dream team for whingers, idlers, prevaricators or prima donnas and if they work well as a team then I'd keep them together as a team for as long as I possibly could and take the work to them.

For more information, watch out for my up and coming thriller – 'Why Resource Pools Never Work' or my articles in Managers of Yesterday entitled 'Matrix Management Sucks' and 'Waterfall Is The Only Way'. No seriously, please don't search for these as I just made them up.

**5** – This is reserved for the World Performers of the Year. I don't seriously think that you can be a 5 on too many occasions. You really must have done something stunning. Either that or the mark is being used tactically to get you more money or a promotion. You may be a superstar for a short while but watch out as it's not sustainable. Your 15 minutes of fame await you but an initially adoring fan club have already clenched their teeth and sharpened their knives with a cunning plan to knock you off your pedestal. It's a British thing!

So they are the numbers and I hope everyone is still with the plot. Hopefully we now all understand my interpretations, whether you agree with them or not.

It's now time to face the music.

Imagine your I.T. organisation were the sole invitees to an all-expenses paid party at a top London nightclub, Tramp for argument's sake. It would have to be compulsory attendance wouldn't it, to get more than 6 people showing up, so a bit of bribery may have to be done in the background. So let's take a few moments to observe the behaviours at the party and analyse the results as they come in.

**The 1's** simply haven't turned up. They are nowhere to be seen as they went to Tramp in Osaka, Japan. No change there then as they were in the wrong place, in the wrong time zone but watch out for those expense claims. No-one, absolutely no-one, should be surprised that this happened.

**The 2's** have formed a nice little clique and have already character-assassinated every single 3, 4, or 5 within a 100-mile radius and metaphorically strung up the DJ. They will only dance 'en clique' and only twice. Once when Sinatra sings 'New York New York' and again when the ubiquitous 'Hi Ho Silver Lining' by Jeff Beck blasts through the woofers and tweeters. They will eat all the food, drink all the champagne and complain all the way home and for most of the next month about how boring it was and bemoaning that they should have been paid overtime for attending.

**The 3's** are enjoying the food, drink and music. They are very comfortable and have managed to acquire the tables furthest away from the DJ in the dim and distant hope that the I.T. Director, who now has his tie masquerading as a headband, doesn't come and ask them to dance.

**The 4's** do not need a table. They all got up to dance straight away and will not sit down again until after the last dance is saved for them. They are floor-fillers not loo-fillers. The DJ loves them, the I.T. Director loves them, the 3's begrudgingly admire them and the 2's hate them with a passion. The 1's think they are 4's themselves but are in the wrong continent so no need to dwell on their views.

**The handful of 5's** have spent most of the evening on the stage with the DJ, selecting the music and inventing new routines to dance to. They organised an impromptu Karaoke session during the buffet break, which they completely monopolised, and invented a new cocktail for the DJ called the Bright Spark.

The real challenge and moral of the story after all of this merry banter is how do we get more 3's to dance of their own individual volition and become the 4's of tomorrow? Having spent many long evenings articulating this analogy, I usually have to have a lie down at this point and contemplate why on earth I should even think of relating something like this ever again.

I haven't a single clue as to what the answer to the problem is by the way, and would be at my holiday home in the Hamptons right now if I did.

If pushed, I would ensure each 3 has challenging objectives, incentives for doing quality work without looking like a caped crusader, a permanent self-managing team to be part of and a damned good coach to really bring them out of their comfort zones. This is proposed on the basis that about 10% may make it, but it's 10% more 4s than you would have had, if you had not challenged the status quo.

# THE BOSTON I.T. PARTY

**Q:** Next year our Company will be organising a champagne celebration for its I.T. department on HMS Waterfall in the City of London. They've done a great job this year and our CEO wants to reward them with a big party next year. What I need are suggestions on the background music we should play in the 30-minute interval. It would be great if you could select 5 tracks that I can dedicate to I.T. and once you have chosen them, let me know why?

**A:** I just love a distraction. It will be my pleasure but please excuse any hint of flippancy as it is a party after all.

My first choice is 'Road to Nowhere' by Talking Heads. This is dedicated to all I.T. people working on large sequential projects without any requirements, plans or sponsorship. I hope the numbers falling into this category are low, but I suspect otherwise.

My second choice is 'We Don't Need Another Hero' by Tina Turner. This is dedicated to all the frustrated and angry people out there who are working brilliantly in total chaos but are infected with the highly contagious Highly Rewarded Hero Virus.

I suggest we calm things down next with Johnny Mathis singing the 'Twelfth of Never' for my third choice. This is for everyone still working on ridiculously large projects, with hundreds of resources, ill-defined scope, no appetite for change or risk, new technology and totally lacking in supporting methods, processes or a scintilla of senior management direction. If this sounds familiar then the implementation date is in the song title. You are on a quest and quests will be ready when they're ready as no-one has the guts to cancel or redirect them.

Let's up the tempo a bit as the food disappears with 'Shout to the Top' by The Style Council for my fourth choice. This is for everybody on the sharp end of a management culture that believes that everything can be achieved by shouting, bullying and traditional command and control structures.

I've never witnessed a project success purely based on the amount of shouting performed by senior management. If you have then please let me know and we'll organise a conference on the subject. I nearly selected 'Shout' by Lulu for this slot but it is not a song that I want playing when

I'm trying to eat vol-au-vents as I tend to make a bit of an embarrassing mess.

To finish off I have chosen 'Looking After No. 1' by the Boomtown Rats. Let's face it if you don't, who else will? It is each individual's career so they need to own it and not expect someone else to make things happen for them.

On a more general point, remember from the Dance Hall Analogy that the 3's won't dance but they will tap their fingers and stamp their feet. However they will neither agree nor disagree with the choice of music – so please expect a level of disgruntlement from them with my Dessert Island Discs.

There are hundreds of different selections I could have made and I hope I haven't offended too many purists with my choice of music. I would like to think I have offended some though!

## THE DREADED DEADLINE

**Q:** I have just been promoted to project manager as the previous incumbent was fired for not agreeing to an imposed delivery date on a critical project. I've told my new bosses that I think it can be delivered to the original deadline with extra effort from the team. Given that is exactly what they wanted to hear, I'm sure I did the right thing, I think. What do you think?

**A:** You sound like you used to be decisive but now you're not sure at all. You will need to provide me with a tiny bit more information but reading between the lines I think I can see what's going on here. Let me try and hazard a few intuitive guesses.

1. I like to work with some data, even small amounts. If the previous job holder had worked out a plan with his team and come up with best case, most likely case and worse case estimates and the best case, even with significant scope compromise from the stakeholders, was still not achievable, then he or she has a good case for constructive dismissal. You can't be fired for doing a professional piece of work – it's the law!

2. Is the imposed date the result of a regulatory change? This is unlikely as the authorities usually give plenty of notice. Maybe an external commitment is driving this. It's not out of the question as executives do go to lunch and do have meetings with City folk, sometimes even without consulting their I.T. department beforehand! It could be as simple as a huge slice of macho management pie.

3. Have the business been advised to strip the requirements to absolutely must-have bare bones and having done this, were options given and risks clearly articulated around each option? Sometimes this is the only way to get a positive outcome and even better if the customers prioritise the requirements into small releases based on their value to them.

I would strongly encourage you to investigate each of the above scenarios as a matter of urgency. It may be too late as you have already committed to the powers that be that you can deliver but you really, really need to understand what this commitment is based on.

31

If you have simply satisfied the whims of an idiot or tried to protect your newly acquired status, then I'm afraid I will have to bet a lot of money on Bound to Fail, the clear odds-on favourite in the first race at the I.T. Asylum. If you have pressed number 3 above and have been placed in a queue with the full and certain knowledge that your input is valuable then you have a fighting chance of snatching victory from the jaws of a complete and utter disaster.

Hopefully you will now realise what you should have done. By now you almost certainly know what you have done. There may even be an outside chance that they are one and the same thing. If that is the case then fantastic, well done! However, if they are different and you have agreed to an end date without detailed analysis of the data at your disposal then you are between a rock, another rock and a third rock.

This is the outcome that awaits you and it's not a great place to be: -

(a) Let's play a game called 'Guess whose date it is? **Clue A:** It's neither the I.T. executive team's date nor the business sponsor's date. **Clue B:** In case you haven't guessed what it is yet then **IT'S YOUR DATE.** It is lighting the skies in flashing lights above your office building and only astronauts orbiting the dark side of the moon can't see that **IT'S YOUR DATE.**

(b) If the original well-planned but unacceptable outcome was arrived at with diligent work from the project team, after a number of intensive sessions with the domain experts, then what credibility will you have if you have committed to an impossible date based on no data at all and without consulting them?

The correct answer, donated free of charge by Captain Metrics who wins two tickets to a Function Point Counting marathon in Siberia, is **NO** it can't be done, this is **WHY** it can't be done, this is what we **CAN DO** by this date and these are the inherent risks we **SHARE.** Oh, and by the way, my team must be responsible for agreeing every single I.T-related decision made on this project in order to protect the delivery date and maintain their commitment to it. Cop that!

There's another curved ball to look out for. There may be some business people who used to work in I.T. that may try and derail the commitment by huffing and puffing with a synchronised shaking of heads. Please control the inclination to shout at them. Simply thank them for their input, but make it absolutely clear that their opinions are all that they are, opinions, and they have no status today. This usually gets a reaction.

If you can manipulate the situation so that the revised and re-negotiated outcome is agreed to by all stakeholders, then you have a successful result and a possibility of winning and if you deliver on these promises then you will be transformed from an I.T. frog to become a Prince too! Come on everybody, what do you expect on a freezing cold January morning - comedy?

## DIATRIBES 'R US

**Q:** Is there anybody in I.T. who can simply answer any straightforward questions without analogies about swimming pools or extensions or types of brick? I am particularly furious about one I heard recently about coffee. It's a diatribe and complete nonsense. Can you stop it now?

**A:** Well who got out of bed on the wrong side this morning? I make no apology for the coffee analogy as it's probably something to do with speaking from practical experience, as opposed to writing a book about surfing but never having actually been in the ocean. This of course is yet another extremely annoying and analogous view.

I particularly enjoy the instant coffee analogy as it really sums up, in an analogous sort of way, what a lot of senior business people think I.T. should provide as a service. How many more times can I use the word analogy?

It's actually not about instant coffee at all but more to do with the performance of the vending machine that dispenses it.

The legend goes something along these lines.

Once upon a time, there was a trader in a big city firm who shall remain nameless but for the sake of argument let's call him Bob, mainly because that was his name. Bob was asked what he would really like his I.T. department to do for him. His first choice was rejected outright due to its physical impossibility, even for those made supple by regular Yoga or Pilates sessions.

What he did say though was this. 'I would happily settle for my second choice. I want my I.T. department to be like the office coffee machine. I insert my card, I order white coffee without sugar, it deducts a fixed amount from my card, it delivers white coffee with no sugar and takes exactly 17 seconds, like it originally said it would'.

For Bob this equates to a successful outcome as it delivers exactly what he asked for. The scope was covered by the delivery of white coffee without sugar. It was spot on budget at a fixed pre-advertised cost, which was exactly what he expected to pay. It was delivered on time, in

34

17 seconds, which is the time he spent scratching his rear end waiting for something to happen.

Even though the coffee was disgusting, this was acceptable given that great tasting coffee would be construed as gold plating and subject to a complex and over-engineered solution. It would also have cost a lot more and that was unacceptable to Bob, who simply could not afford it and even if he could, didn't feel it was worth the investment.

So the moral of the story is that you can always bring Bob to a coffee machine but he can't always afford what he likes best.

The world could do worse than have a few more Bobs in it!

# E

*'**Experience** is the name everyone gives to their mistakes' – Oscar Wilde*

## THE PURSUIT OF EXCELLENCE

**Q:** In my company there has always been a strong focus on excellence in Project Management and the development community have always been a little on the back foot as a result. In spite of this, we carry on with our goal of building centres of excellence in software design, build and testing using improved ways of working. Is it worth it?

**A:** Absolutely, given that on most projects the development phases or iterations consume a fair chunk of the budget despite ill-informed attempts to push a lot more of it towards the analysis phase. It also represents the work that most I.T. departments are good at, despite many expensive failures trying to make case tools and code generators work.

I would like to see a lot more focus on creating first-class development centres of technology accompanied by contemporary methods. It doesn't matter what they are based on as long as the customers get the service they need. History tells us that customers usually get an I.T. department that they deserve.

To take this a stage further, consider the following: -

1. Make sure you have access to specialist domain expert designers.

2. Back these people up with specialist business domain experts who are also available to you when you need them. Ideally co-locate them with the I.T. designers but this is not always practical or desirable.

3. Get as many resources as possible that can estimate and track their own work effectively. If not, train them up so they can.

4.  Have at least one expert in agile and lean methods. Don't be frightened to experiment in your quest for improvement and cross-train as many of your team as possible, so you are not reliant on one or two key individuals.

5.  Make sure your customers are fully aware of their responsibilities in order to get most benefit from these initiatives such as review time, question time, sign-off time and workshop attendance. Changing resources mid-stream is expensive and becomes orders of magnitude more so as you progress through to delivery.

6.  Implement Product Quality Reviews on key deliverables and get as many defects as possible removed before test. Ensure you keep the data from these reviews so that action can be taken to continuously improve the process. Train everyone in the process and make sure it is not over-engineered to such an extent that it loses credibility.

7.  Automate as much of the testing as possible and include all levels of testing. Invest in tools and use any unused system resources to execute tests. Regularly re-build the release, project or work package so there is always something to ship somewhere via a slick release process.

8.  Identify any re-use opportunities early but don't waste your time looking into future re-use opportunities as it will lose you all the time you have gained by working more efficiently on the current project. It's difficult enough delivering to today's requirements without the added complexity of guessing tomorrow's.

9.  Ensure each team actually operates as a team in everything it does. They must support each other and have collective objectives as well as personal objectives. Don't just assume the team only needs training and coaching in estimating, planning, tracking, design, development and testing. Look at the softer skills such as influencing and negotiating. Ensure the team creates and maintains its own asset library to make available the current best practice and lessons learned to everybody.

10. Take some risks. Obviously agree them with your sponsor but don't simply come up with a risk log showing things that may

happen. Include some stuff that will happen and spell out what the consequences are, but also the benefits that can be gained if all goes well.

If you attack some of these areas in a co-ordinated fashion you will be on the road to achieving excellence. This will free up the project managers to do what they are supposed to do and manage more projects simultaneously, with a focus on activities such as stakeholder management and resolving issues. Create an environment where outstanding work is encouraged and rewarded. Throw away the command and control structure and build quality systems for your customers using talented, creative and trusted people.

# ENTERING THE DRAGON'S DEN

**Q:** I am convinced there is a proposition whereby a successful software development and testing enterprise can be established onshore without the need to go totally down the offshore route. What do you think the chances are of success?

**A:** It's eminently doable but there are many avenues to explore even before you do any up-front business case modelling. It's not just about the pitfalls but evolving your strategy to overcome them. Here are just a few things I've thought of but the bottom line is this - if you are passionate about making this work and are in a financial position to do so, then go for it. Do your homework diligently, ensuring all of the figures add up and the outcomes are realistic and achievable.

This is the approach I would take.

(i)     Build a strong business case. Get some help doing this, from both a financial and presentational perspective to make sure it looks professional, has been well thought through and the return on investment is clear and demonstrable to any potential investors, as they need a clear exit strategy as well as an entry point.

(ii)    Decide on your location and what operating model you want to run. Will all work be performed onshore or will you consider taking some tasks offshore? Look into entrepreneur friendly areas that are no more than a few hours travel time to your prospective customers. This is very important. Customers like to see their suppliers on a fairly regular basis and some enterprise boards are happy to assist with early funding in buildings, recruitment and training. Let's face it, you will be viewed as a creator of local jobs, so will quite rightly be treated fairly and hopefully in a positive light.

(iii)   How are you going to fund your enterprise? Bank loan; enterprise boards; venture capitalists or maybe a mix and match of all these. Hopefully you will not consider your life savings or personal assets as the only source of major funding but you will get a good response from potential investors if they see that you are willing to invest some of your own time and money in the venture.

(iv)     What is your unique sales proposition? Why would anybody want to do business with you? What are the benefits over the offshore model? You must crack this nut as many organisations simply look at the cost equation when making an outsourcing decision. Although important, it shouldn't be the only factor but often is, especially in difficult times.

(v)      Build your marketing strategy with care. Do your research so that you really understand what the markets need, how you can satisfy them and most importantly, what they can afford. How much interest can you generate? Are there any particular gaps in the market that you can exploit? Where will your customers be located? What's the competition doing?

(vi)     Decide if you are going to focus on one particular sector and design exclusive product and service offerings for it. The alternative is to acquire knowledge in multiple domains. This can be expensive and will spread you very thin in the early days. A word of warning from experience. Never put all your eggs in one customer's basket. If it gets into trouble then you are in trouble with it. It is a delicate balance but you must strike it.

(vii)    What is your recruitment strategy? What's the balance between age and experience versus permanent or contract people? How will you maintain a steady flow of resources? How will you retain them? Is there a first-class university nearby? Are the graduates generally loyal to the area you wish to locate in and rarely move away if the employer is attractive to them?

(viii)   Devise a competitive pricing strategy. You will struggle to match the offshore units on price alone but you may be able to strike a balance that is attractive. You already have an advantage if you are in the same time zone. You will not suffer any potential issues around communication and you will be able to augment existing staff on the customer's site without concerns about visas or work permits. This doesn't mean you should avoid forging partnerships with offshore suppliers as it will extend your coverage of the working day – just don't have offshore resources onshore – it's very costly.

(ix)    Some ideas for your consideration could be around risk and reward contracts based on high productivity and good quality. How will you measure and demonstrate success to all your stakeholders?

(x)    Consider working with small-to-medium sized enterprises that have some track record of success in competing with the big boys and are quite well established. This can be a software development company or a consultancy that is interested in offering development solutions as part of its portfolio of services. Evolve a pricing model that will be attractive to all parties.

(xi)    Don't be too narrow in your thinking. If you have a prospect that wants you to develop and own a product for them, then don't just dismiss it. It could become a good entry level and will give you a good case study on which to build up your marketing material. It will also potentially provide some much needed cashflow into your company while you are building up your business.

(xii)    Be aggressive in your drive for excellence. Most offshore suppliers are high maturity organisations and you should aim to match this, not necessarily by achieving a certain level of maturity but always focus on delivering value and keeping customers happy. Make this commitment a key part of your initial investment strategy. How about fixing defects for free. OK a bit revolutionary maybe but it will certainly focus the minds of potential customers and give them something to chew over.

(xiii)    Work with local universities and see if they would be willing to review their technology courses to include an element of quality, smart working practices and more contemporary ways of working. Just imagine what you could offer if your developers arrive in your company armed with techniques in how to plan and track their own work as well as remove defects and wasted effort. You will have the basis of a very compelling offer, a competitive edge and a unique sales proposition.

This is by no means an exhaustive list as I'm not that clever, but hopefully it gives you some insight into the challenges to be overcome. Outsourced development is a multi-billion pound minefield. If this was just a price argument then you would struggle to come up with many alternatives. However, it's also about great quality, high productivity, delighted customers and enthusiastic people, which to be honest, many companies, particularly large internal organisations, struggle to attain.

In summary then: -

- ✓ Be passionate about your goals; if you want to make it work, you will.
- ✓ Understand what can go wrong and what personal impact this will have.
- ✓ Devise unique offers that your prospects will find absolutely compelling.
- ✓ Get the cost, quality and delivery precision triangle just right.
- ✓ Make yourself an exciting prospect as an employer.
- ✓ Get your funding sorted up front and have an exit strategy for both investors and yourself.
- ✓ Ensure your marketing material clearly articulates your company's DNA.
- ✓ It can work, it should work and I'm sure it is working somewhere so make it happen and strive to do great things!

# THE OLD ESTIMATING CHESTNUT

**Q:** Every time we produce estimates for a business case we are then held to them for the duration of the project, assuming it proceeds. We are not allowed to factor in any contingency so we end up over-estimating every task so we can meet our delivery objectives. Surely there is a better way of working with our customers than this?

**A:** Mmm... you have identified a problem that is so pervasive in today's cut and thrust project world that I find it amazing that both customer and supplier can't get their heads around how ridiculous this situation really is and fix it.

I believe some progress has been made whenever agile methods have been adopted and projects are developed as more of a joint responsibility. However, I cannot confess to being an expert agile practitioner so I will answer the question from my extensive experience on the more traditional project methods.

First of all, from a customer perspective, what can they possibly hope to gain by asking you to commit to something before you've done any up-front analysis or high-level design work? This is insane. I can't imagine a car manufacturer committing to the cost of their end product without detailed specifications around engine size, colour, chassis size, type of upholstery, audio systems and any other bells and whistles. So why on earth is I.T. being asked to?

This is bad practice from the customer for demanding it in the first place and from the supplier for accepting it without a dogfight or at least demanding an opportunity to explain how the process should work and how estimating accuracy refines as the project progresses.

Estimates can only ever be the estimator's point-in-time best guess based on the data available. For example, at the business case stage, unless you have a large amount of historical data that you can use as a comparison to come up with something meaningful, I would imagine you have at best 50% confidence in your estimates. Despite the insanity of not being allowed to include any contingency, you really must calculate it, incorporate it and be prepared to defend it.

At the start of requirements gathering you will need to secure a budget that reflects your level of confidence in the estimates. For example, if the most likely estimate for the analysis phase is 3 person months then you must secure budget for 4.5 person months if you only have 50% confidence in the estimates and show this explicitly in the schedule. If you are asked to remove it then escalate this to your project board, prepare a presentation to defend it and add it to the risk log until someone comes to their senses and is at least willing to have some debate.

Also consider risk contingency funding that reflects the likelihood and impact of risks materialising and the subsequent cost impact on the project if they did. For example, if you have a credible risk that has a 10% chance of materialising and the total cost to the project would be £100,000 if it did, then you need to acquire 10% of this otherwise there's little point in calculating the figure in the first place and the whole process of risk management becomes a complete waste of time.

'Push back on I.T's estimates' is a common customer chant. 'I.T. are trying to pull a fast one yet again with their usual behaviour of coming to work every day of the week just to make our lives a misery!' And on it goes.

One solution to this eternal problem is to make the use of contingency a project board decision, before any contingent funds are spent. This means that a steering group comprised of both experienced **I.T. and business** people can make an informed decision together. If the contingency is not spent at the end of a phase then a decision can be reached to either give the budget back to the sponsor or recommend moving some or all of it to later phases.

If, however, it has all been spent then it is a sure-fire certainty that the rest of the project is probably in need of a review and a complete re-estimation as the plan will be suspect and potentially undeliverable. This may require more funding or de-scoping and the business case will almost certainly require re-authorisation to see if it still stands up in court. It's a difficult conversation but not one that should be avoided.

So surely it is patently obvious to even the most cynical sponsor that the question that should be asked is not whether we allow any contingency, but how much? This is sensible, pragmatic and professional. No matter how good you are there will be unforeseen and unplanned activities that will plague your project and in times of trouble, everyone wishes they had allowed for some contingency.

Nobody is perfect so the estimates will not necessarily be spot on and you will be impacted by the occasional resignation, unplanned absence or resource not coming on board when they should. This is what contingency amounts should be used to counteract. To simply remove it without any consideration is negligent, stupid and unprofessional!

As the project progresses, you should see both the cost and risk contingencies reducing over time if it is being managed properly. So try and link the cost contingency to the confidence you have in the estimates throughout the lifecycle. Just as an example this could be 50% at analysis, 25% at design and 10% as you start to build the solution. It depends entirely on the project attributes and whether it is brand new or tried and tested stuff you are building.

Having hopefully given you an insight into a possible approach to the thorny issue of contingency and the business concern that I.T. will always invoke Parkinson's Law and any other excuse that can be thrown into the pot, let's have a quick look at estimating.

There are some great books, courses and expert consultancy available on this subject and I am far from expert so I'll just focus on good practice that has worked for me in the past, mainly through trial and error but definitely from use on projects.

- Try and find some credible historical data in which to get a ballpark figure you can work with from the outset. If none exists, find a domain expert and start collecting useful data from then on. If you don't have a domain expert, use a Work Distribution Model. For example allocate. 20% of the effort on Requirements; 25% on Design and so on and then incorporate higher contingency amounts. Ensure estimating confidence is reflected in the appropriate risk profile if you have major concerns.

- Always size the software you are going to build. This is very important. Unlike some other areas in life, size actually does matter. I would recommend that you look at something like function points, number of features, number of requirements and calibrate the outcome with a complexity factor. Estimated lines of code won't cut the mustard as you will be penalising well-written code. Code is also produced far too late in the lifecycle and you need a reasonably accurate estimate much earlier. In any case the estimate could only ever reflect the activities carried out in approximately 30% of the project, and that's not good enough.

- Always give banded estimates with Best Case, Most Likely and Worse Case. I would guess that most projects come in somewhere between Most Likely and Worse Case or later, so bear this in mind. Calculate your contingency amounts based on the Most Likely Estimate.

- Document your estimating assumptions. It may be necessary to recreate the estimates or part of them from scratch due to unforeseen circumstances. The new estimator must know on what basis the original estimates were arrived at, to avoid any issues emanating with the project stakeholders caused by new and nasty surprises.

- Use more than one technique to arrive at the estimates, particularly for larger projects. These techniques can be by Analogy, Expert Judgement or more in-depth methods such as Wide Band Delphi – I'm sorry you will need to look this up folks if you want more detail. This will help you to validate and negotiate prior to arriving at a realistic banded estimate that can give you the required air cover and be defended.

- In a waterfall environment, never commit to an estimate unless you have completed detailed requirements and performed some high-level design. It's just wasting everybody's time otherwise. Once you're ready to commit, baseline the plan and schedule and go for it.

- Always include a level of contingency for unforeseen events or poor estimating but NOT for Change Requests. These must be processed separately and if approved, added to the schedule only when any additional funding and subsequent revision of dates is agreed. Of course you could be controversial and drop some existing scope of equivalent value to protect the original commitments.

- Calibrate your estimates as you go through the lifecycle based on your latest experience on the project. Your schedule should always reflect your best guess and never be more than a week out of date.

- If you can, build or buy an estimating tool that will gradually capture your organisation's estimating and sizing capability. There are some cost-effective tools available but I must stress the need to calibrate them to reflect local practice. Estimating is a competency you will always need to have, so treat it almost like a profession in itself, but never let any tool or averages totally drive the outcome.

- Involve the whole team in the preparation and ongoing status of estimates. This will ensure their continued commitment and result in a positive working environment.

- One final golden rule that may be a difficult pill for some to swallow. The person allocated to the task, estimates the task and not the project manager. By all means challenge but the estimator's word is final.

These are the main areas to address and improve upon. The ideal end game is to get each person's capability factored into the schedule. This will require a culture that encourages people to record their time accurately without fear of being beaten up at appraisal time because they got it wrong. If they are beaten up then guess what, smart people will manipulate the data and the whole thing will fall into disrepute. Nothing will ever get any better.

Do it right and you will get it right and if your actual effort achieves +/- 10% of planned effort then you are doing world-class estimating and your customers will be delighted with you as they can plan their activities based on a position of strength instead of doubt.

# THE EMPOWERED ORGANISATION

**Q:** I have just returned from a communications event that was held off-site in some drab airport hotel where we were told that we were empowered or something like that. What on earth were they talking about?

**A:** Very short answer on this and trust me on this one, you are not empowered. Let's start by discussing what I think empowerment is from a project perspective, although I'm sure it applies equally well to other lines of business.

Empowerment is devolving accountability for decision-making to the project team who then operate within a clear Terms of Reference without the need to defer to senior management for approval on every major decision on the project. The team have the remit and the budget to deliver the solution without fear of failure and with full support of management. In other words, everything is down to the team **BUT** senior management will be there to support when needed. That's the theory but what's the practice?

Does this feel like the way it is in your company? From what you've inferred, I doubt it very much as you hadn't a clue what the presenter was getting at. Sadly, senior management often do what has probably been done to you and used the E-word as a means of abdicating responsibility and every time something goes wrong the answer is usually 'You wanted empowerment, you've got it, so you sort it out '.

Empowerment fails unless backed up by clear communication, mentoring and a commitment to provide **trained** coaches to help you implement it. You simply cannot go home on a Friday evening, take some medication over the weekend and come in on a Monday morning with a spring in your step, whistling 'Empowerment is a many-splendoured thing'. Don't get me wrong, as I'm all for it and it works astonishingly well in small organisations where many things are usually decided at a peer level and always at the informed level.

It is a refreshing culture and is a super way of working and once institutionalised, it adds enormous strength to an organisation's capability. However, to make it work you need an outstanding leader and new ways of working that devolve decision making to the project team. In my experience, sadly, this is as common as hen's teeth.

**F**

*'Success is the ability to go from one **Failure** to another with no loss of enthusiasm' – Winston Spencer Churchill*

## TO FREELANCE OR NOT TO FREELANCE - THAT IS THE QUESTION.

**Q:** It really infuriates me that we have so many contract freeloaders in our I.T. department. They charge outrageous fees and stay forever. I think we should get rid of them all. They earn too much and deliver too little. Well that's what we permies all think. Why is this?

**A:** Well we've had a whinge about consultants in an earlier question so we might as well square the circle and have a go at another group who doesn't meet with the approval of the permanent members of staff.

If there is a problem with having too many contractors then it can hardly be their fault, can it? Unless of course all of the contractors arrived en masse one morning, organised a coup d'état, selected the plum assignments, awarded themselves significant rate increases and automatic renewals forever.

Now I doubt very much whether that happened. If there are so many of them delivering such little value then management are being lazy by not getting rid of them. They must have hired them in the first place. There must have been a reason – good or bad!

My advice to you would be to take the 'If you can't beat them, then join them' approach, or to be more blunt 'Put up or shut up! Generally in the cut and thrust world of corporate life I find that those who can, do and those who can't do, simply moan about those who can.

So why do organisations use contractors? Is it to manage peaks and troughs in demand? Hopefully yes! Is it because the people in the mother ship don't have the skills and experience for a particular piece of work? Quite possibly!

From the contractors' viewpoint, most tend to demand challenging assignments, a fair market rate and variety of work. They have very little in terms of benefits, something that can't be said of the permanent staff. That is their choice and one to be respected.

I apologise to the reader if this comes across as a little bitter and twisted. That's because it is! Contractors don't generally return the favour and spend all day moaning about permanent people and goodness knows they often have good reasons to. No doubt they quietly retain their dignity with the view that having permanent resources in the I.T. department is an acceptable cost of doing business and only ever moan about it in their own time.

## MY I.T'S ON FIRE

**Q:** I am really fed up. My working life is in chaos. Nobody cares about doing things right. Huge fires are blazing everywhere and the firemen are putting them out without wondering why they started in the first place. Can you help me – I'm burnt out!

**A:** I can't believe that nobody cares. The people doing good quality work will care and so will their partners, as they are not getting the benefit of the bonuses being dished out to the fire fighters. Even the partners of the fire fighters will care, as they continually have to refresh their loved ones wardrobes as a result of too many late night pizzas and takeaways. But who started the fires in the first place? Why do we need these people?

Let me hazard a guess – ha ha – get it!

This is outrageous practice often caused by senior people committing to schedules that have not been the subject of much thought, let alone by the team that will actually be doing the work. It's backed up by poor estimating practice and the inability to learn from previous experience. It's made worse by poor tracking of work and having no clue as to where the project is, what state it's in and how or when it will be completed. Complete the recipe with a large helping of inadequate configuration management with people working on the wrong things at the wrong time. Basically it will be some or all of these reasons and almost always when only lip service is paid to quality and delivery of value to stakeholders.

Add to this the inevitable 100-metre sprint to test and you have a nice, shoddy defective product in the making due to inadequate or no quality activities being performed. This is fertile territory for our larger than byte-sized superhero.

Many fire fighters love a crisis, a panic, and a special forces hit and run mission. It's fun, visible, heroic and ultimately their 15 minutes of fame. To be fair, some don't enjoy it but they have no choice. Nothing is ever written down as it's all in the heroes' heads and this breeds over reliance on key individuals. Not only that, with this way of working the fire fighters are often openly rewarded by management, given bonuses, promotions and above all, status.

Those doing quality work, who always meet their dates and objectives, are quite rightly, very angry. It's assumed by all, especially senior management, that their job must be easy as they go home on time having only done 8 hours excellent work, which is absolutely preposterous! The conclusion derived from this behaviour is that these people can be ignored as they only work a 40-hour week and never have to come in at midnight to sort out a problem, as their stuff must be straightforward as it always works.

So what can be done? Unfortunately there's not much that individuals on the team can do but this is what I would suggest the decision makers do: -

- Scour the market and find an exceptional I.T. leader.
- Stop **only** rewarding fire fighting and transition to rewarding quality work as well. This will take time but these heroes are really valuable and simply need to work differently.
- Launch an improvement programme focusing on points of pain and resource it with your very best people, even on a part-time basis. Make sure that everything is geared to improving the outcomes for both your customers and your people.
- Focus on the project management activities first. The technical stuff is usually in reasonable shape but don't ignore it, simply prioritise it.

If executives won't make this happen then consider putting your job on the line for something you passionately believe in. What's the worst that can happen? You get fired, your blood pressure reduces, you get more sleep and your partner cancels the impending split that you have no clue is on its way. Oh and I missed a very small point. It's probably a good idea to get another job lined up first.

# FAILURE – AN OPPORTUNITY TO LEARN SOMETHING

**Q:** Wherever I work it seems to be a common theme that big I.T. projects end up as expensive failures although some of the smaller ones seem to be fine. Why is this?

**A:** Industry data suggests that less is more and small is good; actually it should be small is fantastic. This means small self-managing teams, small budget, small scope, light processes and, if possible, co-located teams who all work together to maximise the amount of work that is valuable to the customer and ignore what isn't of value to them.

I have personally worked on ridiculously large projects and failed spectacularly to get even close to a successful outcome. I do know of people who have delivered large projects but I have never met anybody who either enjoyed the experience or delivered without massive compromises in their business and personal life.

This issue applies equally to externally acquired solutions as well as those developed internally. You would be forgiven for assuming that software packages, where the solution is already built, would not be subject to the same quality and delivery issues but my experience does not confirm this at all.

Although industry data exists that provides detailed reasons for project failure, I think it's only fair that I answer your question based purely on my personal experience. This generally will help to avoid some potential litigation issues arising from copyright abuse.

Small projects and enhancements do not require a rigid method or process and can usually be accommodated by a number of small, self-directing teams with minimal management intervention. There is a clue here!

In my world though, the major reasons for project failure are as follows: -

## POOR INITIATION PROCESS
    (i)      Unrealistic expectations on cost, timescales and size of project.
    (ii)     Ridiculous assumptions such as skilled resources will be available to work on the project as dictated by the project plan. Well they won't be without a superhuman negotiating effort

by the project manager, as they will undoubtedly be tied up on other late running projects.

(iii)    Contingency planning for the unexpected is not allowed by management.

(iv)    Initiation usually takes far too long as not many people really understand that its purpose is purely to mobilise the project and establish a governance structure. Remember that only basic information is available at this stage and this makes any sort of customer commitment nigh on impossible. I.T. must provide their ballpark figures to confirm that the business case is sound but please, please avoid doing the detailed analysis and design during initiation, just to cover your backside on cost and time. Educate your customer as to why this is bad practice and remember the real key to the end date is the start date. Try and limit this phase to 2 or 3 weeks maximum, less would be better and then get on with the project only if all lights are still green or will be greenish with some short, sharp remedial work. It is not a failure to stop a project here. It is a failure to start a project when you are simply not in a position to do so.

## POOR PROJECT PLANNING AND TRACKING

(i)    Incomplete work breakdown structures. Quality controls not scheduled as explicit activities. 'All defects will be found in test as there's no time to do reviews' is the strategy that wins the day but loses the battle – spectacularly!

(ii)    Estimating performed by the uninformed, the inexperienced or the project manager.

(iii)    Unrealistic goals, typically own goals.

(iv)    Roles and responsibilities not defined in sufficient detail. Most people are somewhat bewildered.

(v)    Risks identified that nobody can do anything about. Why not accept them and take the odd risk. Don't completely lose your appetite.

(vi)    Plans not tracked on a regular basis. There is no clue as to where the project is except that it will be on track until the Monday before test is due to start.

(vii)    Nothing is measured, so nothing at all can be managed or learnt.

| (viii) | Resources are either not trained or not available or both. Business and technical domain experts are not available when they need to be. |
| (ix) | All project dependencies are not effectively managed or understood. |

## POOR REQUIREMENTS MANAGEMENT

| (i) | No traceability from source to product deliverables and back to source, so no idea whether the scope has been built-in or not. Testing will struggle, as will User Acceptance. |
| (ii) | No prioritisation. Sometimes you have to take something out that is quite important in order not to compromise the business case. |
| (iii) | No engagement of test, support or infrastructure until it's too late. |
| (iv) | Scope is too big or not broken down into smaller, customer driven releases. |
| (v) | Non-functional requirements are not addressed until it's too late to avoid the expensive re-work required to make the solution perform. |
| (vi) | Ineffective change control of requirements. Change should be expected and encouraged especially when requirements are not known at the start. Rigid adherence to massive requirements documents will result in failure. |
| (vii) | Design and build activities are performed based on assumed requirements and pure guesswork. |

## POOR SUPPLIER MANAGEMENT

| (i) | Incomplete or poorly defined requirements leading to both inaccurate estimating and the wrong product being built. This is particularly true if the build is being performed off-site as the opportunity to fully exploit joint iterative development is not always there. |
| (ii) | Totally misconceived idea that the delivery risk has moved to the suppliers. I will wager a lot of money that this is not the stakeholders' view. |
| (iii) | Inadequate or missing supplier management activities. These include quality assurance, status reviews, health checks, and work product reviews. |
| (iv) | No exit or entry criteria for any deliverables, in or out of the organisation. |

| (v) | Poor configuration management of deliverables. |
| (vi) | A totally unrealistic belief that because a third party is performing the vast majority of the development activities, then the solution will work. Please note that suppliers do not possess superhuman powers or a quality sheep-dip! |

## INEFFECTIVE DEVELOPMENT METHODS

| (i) | Methods are too light or too heavy and not tailored to the needs of the project. |
| (ii) | Elapsed time too long before the customer gets to touch and feel anything. |
| (iii) | Environments are not ready when needed or even if they are, they are not populated with the data needed to make development or testing meaningful. |
| (iv) | Not everyone understands how to develop the solution. People don't know when they're finished or even when they've started. |
| (v) | Recipe book mentality. A far too rigid adherence to a model, framework or methodology which stifles creativity and lowers morale. |
| (vi) | Methods are being developed in-flight during the project causing massive delays while everyone is learning or documenting or waiting. |
| (vii) | Working software is available far too late in the lifecycle. This is the same as (ii) above but duplicated for effect. |

## LACK OF EFFECTIVE IMPLEMENTATION ACTIVITIES

| (i) | Support teams not engaged until it's too late. |
| (ii) | Desired Service Levels are un-implementable due to poor communication of existing constraints or additional budget not being secured. |
| (iii) | No testing of fail-over, recovery or back-up plans. |
| (iv) | No archival functionality built in or planned for future releases. |
| (v) | Inadequate training and familiarisation for all users resulting in lack of sign-off at Go Live; so more delays, more frustrations and more caveats. |

## LACK OF COMMITTED USER INVOLVEMENT

(i)      Requirements not fit for purpose or of quantifiable value.

(ii)     If an existing solution is being replaced, migration plans won't work unless business processes are changed. So what? Change them if it makes sense financially!

(iii)    Expert users are not available or not interested in the outcome. There are no consequences for failure and issues always perceived as an I.T. problem.

(iv)    If the solution is Commercial-off-the-shelf (COTS), the package will not satisfy mandatory requirements as the users were either not engaged in the product selection process or wanted to change it to look like the solution they already have.

(v)     Users not effectively engaged due to logistical nightmares. Sometimes it is better to bite the bullet up front and co-locate as it will be much more cost effective and generate a strong team spirit.

I have given one final thought to your excellent question. If everybody did exactly what they agreed to when the project was initiated then there wouldn't be so many problems. The project initiation document will have taken some time and effort to produce, so the least we can expect is that it is referred to now and again.

# THE FUN TIMES

**Q:** As someone who works to live, I like to work hard but play hard too. What are the funniest or most ridiculous things people have said or done during your career?

**A:** How long have you got? This could easily be the subject of another book. However, as it is my current intention to only write one book on I.T, irrespective of what I may have said in other chapters, I'll give you a few absolute belters but please bear in mind that I am only scratching at the surface and sometimes, to really get it, you simply had to be there.

- 'Shouldn't have failed as it works in production'. This was broadcast loud and clear by the project manager who owned the module that exploded spectacularly when it was used in test for the first time on my project. Further investigation uncovered that:-

  (a) I know it bloody well shouldn't have failed so thanks for that
  (b) There was a data exception caused by spaces in a packed decimal field and my team even highlighted the offending field on the dump and
  (c) It was never intended to release it to production as it was for my project's use only.

  A win treble I think you'll agree. It was one small sentence for man with so much wrong with it for mankind.

- A software defect that resulted in all charges being credited to customers' accounts, caused havoc in a retail bank, although to be fair not with their customers! Crash-scene investigations uncovered a catalogue of disasters accompanied by management words of wisdom such as, 'It couldn't have been tested properly'. Well thanks for that fascinating insight!

  In-depth incident management in the canteen uncovered the actual cause of the problem was a massive chemical reaction between probably the worst database design the world has ever seen and the worst bit of coding since records began. The latter may not be quite true, as I've got a couple of real corkers coming up soon.

The charge amount was held in a signed decimal field - so far, so good? However there was also a Debit/Credit indicator for some bizarre reason, only known to the diseased brain of the database designer in question. Needless to say this confused the life out of the programmer and guess what happened. Yep, somehow in the ensuing confusion, the charge became a credit and all hell broke loose. Stock markets collapsed and there was a run on the dollar. Well actually I made those last two bits up but it was a little embarrassing to put it mildly.

The moral of this story follows. A famous Danish company brews beer. They don't run banks; but if they did, I think they would have run this one and it would undoubtedly be the most popular bank in the world!

- OK, programmers of the world, how about this for a bit of code?
  - Move A to B
  - If A = B Go to Exit
  Why isn't this program doing anything?

- There was a tricky problem with an interest calculation routine so senior management decided to take the code home and have a proper look at it, as they do! After about an hour on the train, the aforementioned senior manager couldn't understand why the comments in the program bore no resemblance to the underlying code. When he arrived at work the next day, he shook the programmer responsible warmly and metaphorically by the throat and asked why.

The answer is unforgettable. 'There's a good reason for that boss. I removed the code but left the comments in just in case I needed to re-instate the code at a future date'. The worrying thing was that a number of people present didn't see this as a problem. Have you ever seen a senior manager turn deep red and then blue at the same time? It's not for the faint-hearted.

# G

*The big secret in life is that there is no big secret. Whatever your **Goal** you can get there if you're willing to work' – Oprah Winfrey*

**GOALS AND THE INNOCENCE OF YOUTH**

**Q:** I am a young obnoxious graduate intake or YOGI and am keen to get my I.T. career off to a flying start. Do you have any advice on what objectives I should be looking to achieve in the next 12 months? My goal is to move into Project Management within a year.

**A:** There's nothing wrong with a bit of ambition but I fear you may be a little aggressive with the timescales. However to your credit you will only achieve greatness if you aspire to it. This is a bit of consultant-ese but somewhat appropriate in the circumstances methinks. My goal has always been quite simple. I aspire to be a little bit better than crap and this attitude has served me well. However a young shaver like yourself may come to the same conclusion in 20 years time but for the moment let's set our sights somewhat higher and have a shot at the title.

So how shall we come up with the objectives?

Human Remains tell us S.M.A.R.T objectives are the way to go, but what does this absurd acronym stand for?

**S** is for Specific not Stupid
**M** is for Measurable not Muddled
**A** is for Achievable not Ambiguous
**R** is for Realistic not Ridiculous
**T** is for Time bound not Tortuous

So why not have a stab at mapping some objectives of your own to the S.M.A.R.T model?

When I was a kid growing up around the Thames Estuary, we would all reach fever pitch every year when the circus came to town. Unfortunately, objective setting in the way it is done in most places I've worked tends to have the opposite effect i.e. time-consuming torture on a grand scale.

It has resembled a circus in some ways though with many a clown, dangerous beast, a few jugglers, several tightrope walkers and one ringmaster thrown in for good measure.

That wasn't very helpful though was it, and whilst I mean no ill-will to enthusiastic young entrants to the I.T. madhouse, a little reality won't go amiss. So here's my acronym that is applicable to all objectives; the S.M.A.R.T nemesis if you like :-

**C-** Always strive to delight your **C**ustomers – they ultimately pay your salary.
**I-** The competence is applied **I**ntellect – be pragmatic and use common sense.
**N-** **N**o, a word much under-used by all; No – we can't do that but we can do this!
**Q-** Put **Q**uality first in every single thing that you do.
**U-** **U**nderstand who all of your stakeholders' are and their wants and needs.
**E-** Always do **E**xcellent work.

OK, I know it's a 6-letter acronym but Cinque is Norman French for 5! Good luck and never forget there is always something you don't know and there's usually a person who's screwed up enough times who can give you some sound advice. Don't be too shy to ask.

Your quest to be an outstanding project manager is a noble one. I've met a few and on each occasion felt they should be stuffed and put in reception for all to admire and pay homage to. They are a rare breed but not yet extinct.

# GAME SHOW HELL

**Q:** I am writing a book on TV quiz shows. Is there a particular show that would appeal to I.T. people and could they possibly win anything?

**A:** Thanks for this. I am always up for a challenge especially ones with an irrelevant, flippant and blind alley flavour. I have hosted a few quiz nights myself and the game they really enjoy is Family Fortunes.

For those of you not familiar with this particular nonsense, it is a contest between two families where each member in turn is asked a question and they have to try and guess the most popular answers given by 100 members of the great British public. My experience tells me that based on past performance, the I.T. families would be lucky to get any points at all. They have been rubbish at the quiz historically but they love the game.

Here are a few examples of the answers they may have given if they ever made it to a live show. Imagine that it's now 20 minutes into a half-hour programme and the latest score between the Engineer Family and the Code Family is 0-0. The TV presenter, who has aged significantly since the start of the programme, moves them into sudden death. This is how it could have gone!

**Engineers:** Name a game you play with a ball. Answer: **Scrum.**
**Codes:** Name the world's most common language. Answer: **Java.**
**Engineers:** Name something Red. Answer: **A COBOL Manual.**
**Codes:** Name any food made from homegrown ingredients. Answer: **Pizza.**
**Engineers:** Name a number you have to memorise. Answer: **356,289,120.**
**Codes:** Name a way of toasting somebody. Answer: **On a spit.**
**Engineers:** Name something made out of wool. Answer: **Cotton.**
**Codes:** Name a word used to describe a very cold day. Answer: **-10° C.**
**Engineers:** Name something that leaves a bad taste. Answer: **A Manager.**
**Codes:** Name something you put out for birds. Answer: **Aftershave.**
**Engineers:** Name something you do before bedtime. Answer: **Eat pizza.**
**Codes:** Name someone you wouldn't see in a disco. Answer: **Bob Jones.**
**Engineers:** Name something with long ears. Answer: **Mr Spock.**
**Codes:** Name a famous TV soap. Answer: **Palmolive.**
**Engineers:** Name a non-living object with legs **Answer: A Tester.**
**Codes:** Name any sign of the Zodiac. Answer: **The V model.**
**Engineers:** Name a type of record. Answer: **A floppy disk.**
**Codes:** Name something you open Answer **A manual.**

**Engineers:** Name something people may be allergic to. Answer: **Planning.**
**Codes:** Name something you'd do on holiday. Answer: **Technical training.**
**Engineers:** Name something that's full of holes. Answer: **Windows.**
**Codes:** Name something you'd wear at a wedding. Answer: **An Anorak.**
**Engineers:** Name something you do in an office. Answer: **Stuff.**
**Codes:** Name something you'd take from a hotel. Answer: **The Curtains.**

At this point, the quiz inquisitor makes a dash from the studio and was last seen sitting on a motorway during the rush hour, stark naked and blowing bubbles.

Although fun, please never darken my doors again, sir or madam. Sincerest apologies to all readers for that ridiculous diversion and we will now get back to the business in hand! Further profuse apologies for those of you now thinking – 'Oh! Do we have to?'

## BEWARE OF GEEKS BEARING GIFTS AND WORDS OF WISDOM

**Q:** I recently attended a software conference in Europe and one of the presentations was full of acronyms and colloquialisms, which were all Greek to me. What does garbage in garbage out actually mean and it would help if you could give me a practical example of PDQ?

**A:** This is very similar to a previous question. However, your question is more specific around GIGO, so is worthy of an entry in the records. I'm also running out of questions starting with the letter G. PDQ is Pretty Damned Quick and used at many meetings by show-offs, consultants and dullards.

What I'll do here is adopt the KISS principle to preclude infuriating you further. The best example of GIGO I can think of is the Road to System Test.

If it's confusing you I apologise but the role of System Test, whatever anybody else tells you, is to independently test the functionality delivered. It is not to mess around in or to arrive at in record time, with no previous quality controls built in to shave off a few pennies. Nor is it to find defects, although it invariably does so by default.

There is irrefutable evidence that shows that the only way to get a half-decent product out of system test is to put a half-decent product into it. Test teams should not allow any old rubbish to be delivered into their environment. Testers need to see evidence of good practice throughout the development phases such as defect removal processes being used effectively or at all, as well as unit test plans and results.

Test teams need to be satisfied that every effort has been made to get the solution in good shape before it is shovelled over the wall to them otherwise it will be garbage in, a defective solution and garbage out, a slightly-less defective solution but defective nonetheless.

Later phases of testing such as User Acceptance and Regression will then probably find some more defects but even with the best test team in the world, a defective solution will be implemented and far more defects than are acceptable will be found by the customer. Hence the requirement for larger than necessary support teams – and on it goes!

A much-repeated message but you simply cannot test in quality. It is particularly important to understand this as many of today's systems are larger, more integrated, more complex and frankly more dangerous than ever before.

You will hear cries of 'Foul' from people who have tested in quality but just ask them the following questions and draw your own conclusions based on their answers.

(i)     How many people were required to support the solution in the first 1, 3, 6 and 12 months of live operation?

(ii)    How long were you executing System Test compared to what was originally planned? What was the cost and time variance?

(iii)   How many defects did you find and what was the breakdown by Severity?

(iv)   What would you change if your job depended on the number of defects found?

(v)    How big was the test footprint – what percentage of the functionality were you actually given the time to test?

(vi)   How did the system perform against the non-functional requirements?

## MR GURU IS IT TRUE?

**Q:** A quick question. In 2005, I had the opportunity to go on an all expenses paid trip by private jet to the South of France for the world premiere of the Da Vinci Code followed by dinner with Ron Howard, the director, (did you know he used to be Richie Cunningham in Happy Days?) and Tom Hanks (did you know he is a famous actor and has even won Academy Awards? – I liked him in Big myself but I didn't really get to grips with the plot).

I also had an invite to have a glass of champagne in Uma Thurman's hotel room but as she wasn't in the film I didn't think that was fair. Well to cut a short story long, I turned down the trip because I wanted to get my hands on a new book on Function Point Analysis. Having reviewed all the web-sites, I found a section called Management Gurus.

So my question is, without beating about the bush, dotting all I's and crossing all T's, taking it off-line, pushing back, setting hares running, opening a can of worms or a mare's nest, running it up the flagpole and see what salutes it, picking any low hanging fruit, playing devil's advocate or generally being boring as an F-word, what is a guru?

Is it an animal and if so, what is it doing in the Software Measurement section of Management Gurus? I've got to go now but please keep your answer short and to the point as I do in everything I do, well I try to, but sometimes it doesn't quite work out and I don't understand why some people run for cover when they see me coming the other way. I can't remember exactly how many wings I picked off insects when I was at school but if you want a banded estimate it was somewhere between 1,256 and 1,258.

**A:** Good Grief! What's all that about? I'll answer the question from the same perspective as you asked it even though it is written in a language that I don't understand and have no wish to. Maybe it's early Esperanto? Please excuse my puerile revenge but you have made me lose the will to live with your question, although on the upside, I am now off the sleeping pills and thanks to you I sleep like a baby with your question tucked neatly under my arm instead of my teddy bear.

You probably don't know this but in Sanskrit, guru means teacher. Another language specifies it in two syllables; gu - meaning shadows and ru - meaning he who disperses them. I imagine you are scratching your head at

66

this point but because of their power to disperse darkness and shed light, gurus have evolved.

Personally I tend to put silver coins in an electric meter, which tends to have the same effect. A management guru, to be serious for a nanosecond, is someone who enlightens us about management stuff. Some 'gurus' actually possess hands-on management experience and these are the ones to focus on, otherwise it's just theory albeit in some cases credible theory.

Anyway must rush, but before I do I'd like to point out that the animal you may have been confusing a guru with is in fact a Gnu (pronounced gernoo). This is also known as the Wildebeest and if the reader is awaiting a point to be made or a punch line then I can only apologise – there isn't one!

# H

*'We can't all be **Heroes** because someone has to sit on the kerb and clap as they go by' – Will Rogers*

## HEROES AND VILLAINS

**Q:** OK so I'm a hero. What's the big deal? I really can't understand why all of a sudden, it's fashionable to say we don't need this type of behaviour. I'm on call 24 hrs a day, 7 days a week and 365 days of the year, much to my wife Lois' annoyance. I get called in at all hours of the night and within a short space of time, the problem is solved and it's back to bed with Lois. Can you shed some light on this anti-hero phenomenon as my cape is getting somewhat dishevelled and a little singed?

**A:** In the 1960's, Brian Wilson wrote a great song for the Beach Boys called Heroes and Villains. Those were the days when young people started to live life a bit differently and computers and technology, although not exactly new kids on the block, were emerging fast as 'must haves' for many companies. In those days, computer programmers used to handcraft code, which ended up as punched cards and paper tape for the operations staff to compile and run for them.

The programmers had nothing else to do all day but to desk-check their code and await the next compile slot. Generally this meant that a lot of the code always worked but it was not the most efficient way of doing business. Then along came inter-active compilers, which started to make us all a little bit lazier although we still liked to walkthrough our code with other programmers in a sort of Jurassic version of Product Reviews.

Then, in the 1980's something dramatic happened to the technology world with the advent of the Client/Server paradigm and distributed applications started to emerge. This was deemed new and sexy and it demanded people who could be creative, wear a baseball cap back-to-front, say 'yo wassup man' a lot and strut their stuff.

In line with the dawn of this new era, solid practices started to take more of a back seat which led to a reduction in software quality. At the same time, almost embarrassingly, the hardware industry started to introduce an order of magnitude price/performance improvement every 18 months or so. This ironically made our newly-defective software products get to market quicker than ever before. Out of these ashes the I.T. hero was born.

Heroes are fire-fighters; they love war zones; they have fun and get their name in lights. However what heroes are not, are the villains. It's their management that are the villains for ignoring the people who work in a disciplined way, write their code, remove defects, do documentation, produce other system documentation for test and support to use, execute their tests as planned, compare their outcomes to expected results and generally deliver a good quality product all round. This was viewed as very dull and 'The Old Way'!

Sadly, 'The Old Way' was also viewed by management as easy and risk-free. The people who worked in this space were viewed as average as opposed to excellent, although as individuals, they tended to be happier and spent more time away from work having a life.

What we must start to do as an industry, is reward this 'easy' work more than we reward the fire fighting and as a result transform our heroes to be the superstars of a better way. We need to change the management culture so it's no longer acceptable to deliver defective solutions and charge customers inflated support costs.

Our heroes are usually some of our most talented people in many ways but management needs to stop only rewarding this heroic behaviour and transfer the bonus pot to recognising excellent work.

If I was you I'd embrace this refreshing change with open arms and become an evangelist for quality work. You'll find that the midnight calls will stop, the waistline reduces along with your intake of pizzas and you can spend more time with the lovely Lois. Help create the new A Team and ignore the death threats from the Pizza company; they'll survive without you.

# THE HIERARCHY DEMOLITION DERBY

**Q:** I have worked for a number of internal I.T. departments over the years and the first thing I always get shown is the organisation chart, also known as the organogram. There are usually several layers of management that I really don't understand the need for. Can you let me know why this is?

**A:** No I can't but I think I understand how they originated. If you have a walk around any large office, on any day of any week of any year, you will see someone updating the organisation chart. I've even heard it called the orgasmogram because it gives so many people a buzz. It can never ever be up to date given the amount of continual change occurring; however that's not your question.

One of the reasons for hierarchies could be a by-product of the armed services way of working. This has infiltrated business as it is the way that most humans think and certainly the only way the forces can operate. Orders are issued and obeyed. Command and control is the only way it can work when you are under fire and outnumbered, but it has no real place in today's business world.

However, the one prevalent criticism being fired at I.T. departments is dissatisfaction from their customers, so a different approach is needed. We must have creativity and managed risk-taking in an environment where self-managed teams operate without the innovation killers – fear and blame.

Major contributors to the sustainability of hierarchies are the performance management systems, or certainly the lack of good ones. I worked in a major financial institution for many years and there were five layers of management or blotting paper to go through before you got anywhere near anyone doing proper hands-on development or support work for a customer. Imagine the cost of this.

This way of disorganising is favoured because the boxes on the ubiquitous charts contain major prizes. For example, to be in Box A you had to have 6-8 direct reports and other such-like nonsense before you collected enough bonus points to qualify for the job size that gave you the next promotion. Further prizes of a higher salary, an office with bigger paintings on the wall, access to higher tier canteen facilities and a better quality carpet were also on offer.

I'm sure things have moved on from here as from a pure financial perspective, it's not sustainable or justifiable. The further up the food chain you go the bigger the prizes you win and these are difficult to refuse.

Now multiply this by several layers and you get a huge hierarchical organisation chart and before you can say company car, you have a major problem on your hands from an efficiency and morale perspective.

Then, a new broom comes in, calls in the International Rescue Consultants for an efficiency review, who then proceed to up-size, down-size, left-size, under-size, many sighs but never right-size. The organisation chart changes again and so it goes on. A full-time equivalent is required simply to communicate all these changes and keep the chart up to date.

The fundamental point I'm making is that if you create a box and fill it with goodies, then predators who aspire to it, will occupy it. This is often encouraged irrespective of the trail of disaster left behind and the additional overheads incurred. Hierarchies to this extreme have no place in any organisation and certainly not in the knowledge industry which is populated by very positive, intelligent people, who if empowered properly and given the environment to be productive, can achieve great things.

The crux of the matter is this and it's a critical point. A manager's job is to create an environment that encourages and rewards outstanding work, whether it is via supply of technology, good practice or people-focused improvements. It is not to do the work themselves or do any estimating or attend meetings on requirements because they've got nothing better to do. It is certainly not to sit in a glass office with the door shut holding meeting after meeting where no white smoke ever appears and certainly no decisions are made of any relevance or if they are, they are never communicated outside of the chosen few. Managers must remove obstacles that are stopping the team's progress and stifling creativity.

I was that soldier in the office many years ago and it took me a very long time to realise that this was nonsense and I had to change my behaviour. However, it takes an outstanding leader to make the change happen because it's not easy and there will be casualties. I was lucky at the time as I think I had one.

The days of command and control are over. Build great teams, encourage and reward outstanding work, walk through walls for your team, let them get on with it and be amazed at the results.

One final thought on organisation charts, just in case you are not convinced. Have you ever wondered why people's eyes are always looking up at the I.T. Director's box and their backsides are usually facing the customers? This explains alot.

# HEALTHY PROJECTS

**Q:** I am running a very large and complex project and thought it would be a good idea to have an independent review of how things are going, as we all sometimes get too blinkered and too emotional the nearer we get to the coal face. This often means that we miss the obvious or become too protective of our actions. So our Quality Assurance function performed a health check but only seemed to observe a few cosmetic issues. As I was charged over 50 person hours for the review, I am not best pleased with the outcome and am thinking of scrapping the rest of those that I have planned. Is this a wise thing to do?

**A:** As the majority shareholder in the health checks, you are entirely within your rights to scrap them if they are not adding any value. The main challenge with any health check is getting suitably qualified and experienced staff to perform them. It is difficult for me to comprehend how someone who has never managed a project, for example, can ever do a health check on one.

You have to have been in the war zone to gain credibility or the outputs will be ignored and the whole process then falls into disrepute. Also, I'd be interested to know whether the people performing the health checks are in the same reporting line as the Project Managers. If so, this lacks independence and the health checker may be compromised over loyalty to the project manager and a 'tell it like it is' health check report will never see the light of day.

If you populate the health check resource pool with people you don't know what else to do with then you are asking for trouble. This may explain your problem.

To achieve the best return on investment you will certainly need: -

- Experienced delivery managers performing the health-check.
- True independence of reporting lines.
- A good, credible process with timescales and deliverables.
- An absolute crystal clear statement on whether the project will deliver to its objectives. Cosmetic errors are of no relevance to the outcome from a customer perspective.

- The recommended actions need to be integrated into the project risk and issues logs and not treated as a separate exercise that just gathers dust.
- An escalation route to senior management is needed if the recommendations are not acted upon within a reasonable and agreed timescale.
- To review all methods and lifecycles in use on the project, the people issues and the working environment. It is simply not good enough to just observe whether a standard process is being followed. The fact that a different font is in use on one section of the requirements documentation will not preclude Go Live. Who cares? An inappropriate way of working will!

Do these properly or not at all.

## HISTORY FEEDS THE NOW

**Q:** Best practice encourages the use of historical data from old projects as input to the estimating activities for new projects. I am concerned about this inasmuch as I have no idea how our existing data was collected and how accurate it is. What do you propose I do as we are embarking on a process improvement programme and are targeting an excellent result (CMMI® Level 2) within a 9-12 month timescale? Frankly I'm worried.

**A:** I'd like to correct some misconceptions if I may. Firstly you cannot use any data for which you have no clue as to its origin or accuracy. This would be ludicrous although this hasn't necessarily stopped people in the past. Secondly, lose the objective of achieving a level in 9-12 months as it's not what you are trying to achieve, trust me! Thirdly, try and lose the words 'best practice' as it discourages innovation; the very best any practice can be is as good as we've managed to improve things up to now.

What I would recommend to start with is to target incremental improvement based on a prioritised set of small to medium sized changes to the way things currently get done, perhaps released on a monthly or quarterly basis. Keep them small and of no more than 3 months duration, much less if humanly achievable or you run the risk of achieving diddlysquat and getting the whole thing canned. Just make sure the customer gets a real deal out of it and it's not just an I.T. driven initiative.

It just so happens that most of the issues today are project management related and therefore can be resolved with a focus on Level 2 process areas. In my experience the jump from 1 to 2 is a massive one and to put a timeframe on it is ridiculous and doomed to failure unless you have exceptional leadership and sponsorship, as well as someone who has done it before with the scars and war stories to back it up.

OK, before I address your specific question on historical data, I think I should provide some guidance on measurement from a CMMI® perspective. First of all, I suggest you take a look at the Measurement and Analysis process area itself to familiarise yourself with what should be done from a good practice perspective.

If you are collecting data today then ensure it aligns with the improvements you are proposing otherwise you won't know whether they are working or not. Also, make sure there is a demonstrable positive impact on your customers and you are not simply satisfying the requirements of the model or the I.T. function, as that is plain stupid!

Can I suggest that you start off with a few simple measures and lose the historical data you have as you have no idea what it is, even though it may well be used by some bean counters to measure whatever it is they measure?

I would start again from scratch and get your project managers and teams to start collecting data on cost, quality and timescales. This will build up over a period of time and will become very useful learning for the organisation in the future.

I also propose that the position you want to get to is where everyone in the organisation is collecting their own personal data so their capability is always reflected in the schedule and estimates. Ideally this would then be shared amongst the team and used to form the plan and schedule. Avoid using averages or guesses from an ill-informed source or estimating tools that are not populated with your data.

All this will take time and again needs strong leadership to ensure the correct data is collected and not used inappropriately. In the meantime, consult the experts you already have in estimating and start collecting some meaningful data and don't make it too complicated. A much repeated warning and this is crucial - never ever use the measurement data to beat up people at salary review time or it will be skewed in their favour as soon as you can say Function Point Analysis really works.

**Note from author:** At this point it is with regret that I apologise to all measurement people for my somewhat disparaging remarks about Function Points. I'd like it to go on record that I do not like Function Point Analysis because most people don't understand it nor want to. However, until such a time that a viable alternative is developed and rolled-out across the industry, I fully accept that this is the only way to accurately measure productivity, size and defect density. Now that hurt!

So to summarise then, historical data can be effectively deployed if: -

- The data is easily interpreted and can be applied to different development tools and methods.

- The source of the data is known and credibility in its accuracy is agreed throughout the organisation.

- Effective management reporting can be produced from it, which enables informed decisions to be made on cost, timescales, size and quality.

- Meaningful commentary is available which clearly articulates the bases on which the data was captured and any assumptions that may have been made at the time of collection.

# I

*'You can't wait for **Inspiration.** You have to go after it with a club' – Jack London*

## IMPROVEMENT – START BY ALL MEANS BUT THE MUSIC MAY STOP

**Q:** Our improvement plans have been put on hold while the new management team settle in and have a look at all internally funded initiatives. Why is it that whenever this happens they always target improvement work? Surely the reasons we started the work in the first place are still valid irrespective of personnel changes?

**A:** It's probably even worse than you think. You may find that pet projects that add little value to the customers carry on regardless and the improvement programme that potentially, if you work on the right things, can deliver a significant return on investment, gets canned or at best postponed for long enough that it will lose all momentum and focus and never recover.

On the bright side though, as the programme is no doubt inextricably linked with a previous regime, it may only be a temporary suspension while the new management team  marks its own territory. This is the best outcome you can hope for in these difficult and somewhat tense and confusing circumstances.

I'm absolutely convinced that if the Board of Directors were more informed as to the value of continuous improvement and could sponsor it more effectively with their time and best people, then their I.T. function would evolve into a tremendous asset.

I appreciate that this is fairly contentious but I believe it to be true nonetheless. Most survivors of re-organisations will take every opportunity to feather their own nest first, within the new regime, and it could be a career-limiting move to be seen to support a previous improvement programme even if they passionately believe it's the right thing to do. I can't really blame them as it takes a brave person to put their job on the line especially if they are totally dependent upon it to maintain their lifestyle.

There is also the ignorance factor to consider. It suits many senior managers to have the view that improvements are a licence to print money and are a waste of time. Their knowledge of high maturity practices and their benefits is strictly limited to a maturity rating and they haven't the first clue or interest in anything else. They miss the end game totally as continuous improvement will bring about cultural change if implemented successfully as well as delivery improvements for the stakeholders. This may well be considered a threat to their safety zone and they don't realise that improvement is a never ending journey not a 'Got the Plaque and the Bonus – job done'.

Remember, it only takes a very short time to document a process, but a significant amount of time, effort, encouragement and commitment to get the improved ways of working deployed across an organisation in a consistent manner. It needs people to move out of their comfort areas and fundamentally change the way they work. This is why a massive percentage of change programmes fail to deliver. It requires talented people and hard, thankless tasks to make them work!

I do sympathise with you as I doubt very much that you are a budget holder and therefore have little influence in any strategic direction. You are basically very limited in what you can achieve without active sponsorship.

Here are some fairly obvious things to look at next time round that may just sway the decision the other way. Even so, improvement will always be a soft target, from a cultural, financial and political perspective as it takes a brave and knowledgeable person to stand up to the cost cutters or new brooms and evangelise the benefits.

✓ Prepare an executive briefing and let the board know what you expect of them prior to doing any work at all. For example, make statements like 'These are your executive responsibilities and if you carry them out then I won't have to continually seek commitment and sponsorship and we will deliver something very special'.

✓ Make improvement a significant financial incentive of the entire management team. They may take a different view then and become less cynical if bonuses are linked to improvement.

✓ Try and ensure that the improvement programme is prioritised alongside other projects in the portfolio. If it has a high net return then it deserves to take its place in the order of merit. Tricky one this though, so be prepared for a tactical retreat or two during this battle.

✓ Make sure you exploit what you already have. This will help with getting the coalface credibility that you need to give the programme momentum. For example, if testing is broken, fix it irrespective of where it sits in a model. Your people know what's broken and what works well, so engage with them.

✓ Prepare a regular release plan for the improvements and communicate it to everyone. People will then know what to expect and it gives them time to challenge the content. It will gain the buy-in so that the transition to standard practice is less painful. Small improvements that are delivered regularly are often much better than going for the whole elephant family in one massive bite.

✓ Try and get everybody to spend a couple of hours a week on improvement, more if you can but not too much. If you have a 7-hour planning day for developing product, reduce it to 6 and use this non-project time on improvement initiatives and track it closely to start with.

✓ Communicate success to your stakeholders. This will give you the air cover that you badly need to really make a go of it via real customer commitment. They may then support you at the next regime change or financial challenge.

✓ Have a visual, easy to understand, colour-coded summary that clearly evidences progress against the critical improvements. Ensure it hits home at all levels and pulls no punches. Keep it up to date and visible.

✓ Continually let all levels in the organisation know what's in it for them. Set measurable and realistic targets and explain what each measure is used for and what difference it will make to the entire organisation if the target is reached. For example, just stating that testing will take less time and cost less money is simply not good enough. By how much is what they will want to know and by when?

I hope this helps a bit but nothing ventured, nothing gained. It is a great shame that improvement is a soft target when the cost-cutting knife slashes its way through the budget. People very conveniently forget that improvement is all about doing things differently i.e. better quality, reducing costs and improved speed to market. Why would any sane person wish to stop it? Well they wouldn't, would they?

# VIRTUAL INSANITY

**Q:** Insanity rules and is alive and kicking in my organisation. Just for my own peace of mind and for a little light relief, can you share with us the most insane things you've encountered during your I.T. career?

**A:** I believe a senior executive is alleged to have said that a ridiculously low amount of memory, 648k or thereabouts, should be all you will ever need although he categorically denies it. That was a pretty good one but tame in comparison to what follows.

With the risk of repeating myself from an earlier question, here are my favourites and when you realise they have been said by reasonably intelligent people, it just makes matters worse or funnier or both.

- 'It's the new way. You don't do design anymore'. An utterance overheard from senior management following the purchase of an expensive CASE tool. It must have been some sort of early artificial intelligence. It was, of course, complete nonsense but set quite a few long-eared animals on the march I can tell you!
- 'Never allow the lack of requirements to prevent you from developing the solution'. I'm sure a complete set was what he meant to say but legends are often made as a result of a missing word.
- 'Let's get into System Test as quickly as possible so our senior sponsor can see us making real progress'. I can't even begin to explain how much is wrong with this, so I won't even try.
- 'I thought the annual I.T. conference was so good that it should be held every year'.
- 'We are building software factories. The first thing we'll do is remove all the phones and only allow e-mails at lunchtime'. That'll work then. People will feel really valued and trusted won't they? I think the point was missed by about a time zone!!
- 'Sorry I can't come in to the office today as I'm allergic to the building'. Probably my favourite sick-note story.
- 'How's it going, George?' 'Fine thanks; we're 90% through the code and 10% through the requirements'. This is an example of George taking the previous bullet on complete requirements a little too far. With hindsight maybe George was an early adopter of agile methods but he couldn't possibly have known.

- 'I don't need to track the progress. I can smell when a project's on schedule'. Really – what a talent!
- 'We're not using contingency on this project. The sponsor won't allow it'. 20,000 function points, 200 man years and a few million quid later, the system testers have their hands on one module, and guess what, it doesn't work. Yippee!!
- 'Yes we can', is the only language I want to hear on this project. An intellectually challenged manager taking positive thinking a little too far.
- 'Our customers are demanding fixed price contracts before the requirements are agreed'. So that's what we'll do as we need to up our customer satisfaction scores.
- 'We can't use a standard development methodology on this programme given there are 7 different companies involved in it'. Well call me old Mr Confused but isn't that exactly why a standard approach is required. The alternative is to have er....7!
- 'This project has been in initiation for 20 weeks and it's our No 1 priority'. No it isn't is it? After 20 weeks we should have nearly finished the build, shouldn't we?
- 'Why is this project called Winchester? Well, if it fails to go in on time the project manager will get shot with a rifle'.
- 'Why is this project called Hull?' Apparently it's where the first workshop was held. It's a good job it wasn't held in Santiago di Compostella.
- 'This is our biggest project for 25 years. That's why we've got a brand spanking new development tool, new methods, new standards, new environments, over 25 senior users in 14 sites and over 100 people, mostly new to the company. Isn't that fantastic?' A nightmare scenario!
- Senior Manager says 'So what's your recommendation for Go Live this weekend?' Project Manager says 'No No No. Under no circumstances whatsoever'. Senior Manager comes back with 'OK team we're going in this weekend. I'll book the flights'. Don't you love it when informed people make implementation decisions?
- 'We don't think Jim is doing a great job running software engineering. He's a bit weak on delivery and the customers hate him with a passion. I know, we'll put him in charge of improvements'. Probably explains more than anything else why improvement programmes fail to deliver most of the time!

## IMMATURITY BREEDS CONTEMPT

**Q:** I commissioned a group of consultants, which I now sincerely regret, to perform a review of my department's project management capability. They reported that we are immature in project management, even though a number of the consultants didn't look old enough to vote. However, before I pay their invoice I'd like your view on what characteristics are displayed by an immature organisation and even then I might make them wait a bit for their expenses.

**A:** Not paying invoices on time is a characteristic of an immature organisation. Immature does not mean people sulk or gloat outrageously whenever they win or lose.

It could even mean that some good practice may exist but it is seldom used, particularly when the heat is on. However, the immaturity church is a very broad one and can vary from totally clueless to fairly sophisticated.

This is why it's a good idea to get some sort of assessment done so you have the basis for a prioritised action plan for improvement and a stake in the ground from which to move forward. In your case it just happens to be the project management arena. So you have done exactly the right thing, albeit your choice of consultants may leave a little to be desired, in your opinion.

Herewith follows some of the characteristics of an immature organisation. How many apply to your shop? Those that do can become the focus of your action plan to remedy the situation but always remember to prioritise those activities that will be of most value to your customers.

- Chaotic working environment; reliance on the A team to recover and deliver every project.
- Management wear fireman's uniforms and nice shiny yellow helmets.
- No learning from previous projects – good, bad or indifferent.
- Projects do not consistently or ever meet goals on cost, time or quality.
- Processes and methods are improvised or written in-flight.
- Existing processes stay on the shelf gathering dust in times of trouble.

- Project Plans are never referred to again after their initial baseline.
- No re-calibration of estimates as work progresses and knowledge increases.
- Contingency is banned.
- Documentation, however brief, is not kept up to date with the latest status.
- Change control is performed in an informal way, frowned upon or not done.
- Management believe tools provide silver bullets to counteract bad practice.
- Reactive – focus on the immediate crises and celebrate when raiders passed.
- Quality activities bite the dust at the first hint of trouble.
- Example of immaturity: 20-week projects stay in Green Status (all on track) until the end of Week 19 – then go Red for 6 weeks (nothing on track – no advance warnings).
- Management never ask questions about quality, stakeholder activity or customer satisfaction – only about the end date.
- Customers don't see anything between requirements agreement and User Acceptance Testing – then they don't like what they see. Massive rework – Loss of Credibility.
- Management think outsourcing removes their risks and issues to a place across an ocean or time zone. So they proceed full steam ahead on this basis
- Absolutely nothing is measured and data is never used to manage the project.
- An unstinting belief that when all else fails, shouting and fear will carry the day.
- Management believe everything can be done over a weekend.
- People are allocated tasks that they don't know how to start or finish or both.
- People are working on tasks that have not been allocated to them; in fact they don't appear anywhere, in any schedule, at any time – ever!
- People are allocated 7 hrs per day on product development. This is fine if they always work a 12-hour day. They need the other 5 hours to do all the other activities that they are being asked to do by their organisation – for some unknown reason.

I think it's best if I stop right here – it's in danger of becoming another rant!

## INFORMAL IS MUCH QUICKER AND CHEAPER

**Q:** I have recently been trained in how to facilitate product review sessions where we collectively attempt to remove as many defects as possible from a project deliverable. I have tried to implement structured reviews on a couple of projects and although they initially met with some enthusiasm, the project managers now want a more informal and quicker way of achieving the same result because they take too long. Have you anything else I can use?

**A:** Yes, as a matter of fact I have. They were successfully wielded by Joe Di Maggio, Babe Ruth and Mickey Mantle and make a nasty crunching sound when applied properly but of course only metaphorically. It's illegal otherwise.

I assume that they want a more informal process because they believe that (a) the formal process is over-egging it (b) it's not very exciting (c) it will add to the budget and timescales and (d) even if defects are significantly reduced, the customers don't care as they need their products delivered on time (whatever that means!).

Can I make a suggestion? Either do them properly or don't do them at all. It takes as long as it takes to be effective. It's like saying to a builder it's OK to use sub-standard materials for the extension because even if it falls over next year at least it was delivered to cost and time, and there's always budget lying around for support or a total rebuild.

Don't just take my word for it. Effective reviews, where major defects are removed early in development, and certainly before test or the customer finds them, significantly reduce costs and timescales. There is a vast amount of data available to underpin this if you are not convinced and need some evidence.

However perception is everything. I passionately believe that it is the project manager and their team's professional duty to get as many defects as possible out of the solution prior to test. I am in no doubt that the quality of any solution has a direct correlation to the quality of the practices used throughout its development.

Work Product Reviews are the most powerful and effective practices you have at your disposal. Training can be provided on Day 1 with all the learning deployed and valuable on Day 2. It doesn't get much better than that.

What are you going to say to your customer? 'Sorry but we left all these defects in on purpose because we wanted to hit our dates and budgets'. Nice try but I guarantee that you will have missed your targets anyway if you haven't performed effective reviews and don't forget your customers are probably not in the game of trading product delivery and quality They will want it all and they will want it now!

The only way to ensure that they get done is to make reviews mandatory for key deliverables and enforce the policy, with or without help from the baseball team's equipment locker! It doesn't have to take light years to achieve a satisfactory outcome. Why not try a few different processes and see what works for you whether it is formal inspections, sampling or a mixture of both. Do whatever the team think is most effective based on the results.

# J

*'Good **Judgement** comes from experience; experience comes from bad judgement' – Frederick Brooks*

## THE JFDI SYNDROME

**Q:** I fully appreciate that the so-called JFDI (just effectively do it) projects are critical to our business customers and must be done. Where I do have a problem is when every project is a JFDI project and this becomes a way of life. Do you have an approach where we can ensure that not all projects are drop-dead urgent and we can be successful when it really is a valid must-do project?

**A:** It's good that you recognise that these types of projects are necessary. Even the risk surrounding these projects could be reduced with a bit more strategic planning and discussion with stakeholders. However, that's not something the I.T. people can really influence so we just have to roll our sleeves up and get on with it. The worse-case scenario is that I.T. spends 2 weeks moaning about things and how hard done by they are and life's so unfair, and then a critical piece of work is delivered 2 weeks late and a market edge is missed.

So in answer to the first part of your question, a little bit better communication as to what's in the pipeline coupled with a robust project prioritisation process would help move things in the right direction. A simple scoring system that takes into account the various aspects of the project, especially net return on investment and value to the stakeholders, would be good with big bonus points for the JFDIs that can only be awarded by seriously senior executive management – the real grown-ups.

Once this is achieved, some proper resource planning can be done covering both availability and skills. Any pushback to the sponsors for a priority call can then be achieved from a position of strength.

'We can do this new urgent project, however this is the impact it will have on the existing portfolio', is a healthy debate that would really be appreciated by the senior executives. What doesn't go down quite as well is 'No we can't do this' without any justification or impact analysis. This is not providing a service. Clear options need to be presented so a sound business decision can be made.

The second part of your question gives me an opportunity to introduce a little food for thought. Most organisations have a lifecycle and method for large waterfall projects. Some forward thinking organisations have the same thing for iterative and incremental development. Some even have a framework for small projects, for argument's sake less than 100 days effort, which are often an important slice of the portfolio pie from the customers' perspective.

I think it would be fantastic to have a lifecycle and methodology for a JFDI project rather than trying to cherry-pick a bit of this and a bit of that and making a complete dog's breakfast of it.

So this is the approach I would take and these are just a few of the things that need to be integrated into the JFDI method adoption. It obviously assumes that the business case stacks up and approval to proceed with the project has been granted before you start.

- Kick-off with a 1 or 2 day project definition event with all stakeholders locked away in a mobilisation workshop. By the end of Day 2, there should be a project approach, plan, cost, risk and issues log, assumptions and dependencies and a timeline with major milestones and deliverables.

- Keep the scope to an absolute minimum. Don't even discuss later phases at this stage as the initial JFDI may well be good enough. Whatever you do, don't try and future proof your solution. It's a waste of time and will negate any productivity improvements you will gain from minimising the JFDI scope. By all means list other requirements and put into a pot for later discussion and prioritisation but even then, if you run out of time simply don't bother with them. So manage expectations with your stakeholders and don't commit to anything other than the minimum to ensure a successful outcome for everyone.

- Ask the customers to prioritise the requirements using the MoSCoW approach, or something similar, to validate the previous bullet point i.e. segment the requirements into Must Haves, Should Haves, Could Haves, Wait and sees. Only commit to the Must Haves as these must have a real quantifiable value to the business and investigate ways that some function can be delivered as soon as it's ready i.e. short, sharp and sweet.

- If humanly possible use an iterative approach so all stakeholders can see what they're getting as soon as possible. Build and deliver a working solution as soon as you can to get the show on the road and preclude possible misunderstandings.

- Never skip peer reviews of the key deliverables. Simply run tighter meetings and focus on the major defects. You will save so much time later on in testing.

- Make sure your team meetings are more regular than weekly, at least in the beginning. Keep gaining that commitment from all resources to deliver to plan, and come up with good ideas for reducing time without compromising quality. You will at some point have to take some risks, so think about what they might be and share them with your stakeholders.

- Look at your environment requirements and release management process and come up with a way that they can be fully optimised to fit the needs of the JFDI project. Consider daily builds and data refreshes. Ask whether testing can be further automated to use as much as possible of the 24 hour day. Can you build any test harnesses so testing can start early? In other words, think outside of the traditional method toolbox!

- Make sure your project continually executes like it's a Red or failing project. Why not start it off as Red and try and make it Green by the end of the project as it progresses through the Green criteria. JFDI requires different behaviour. It always puzzles me when a project goes Red and its way of working simply never changes from when it was supposedly on track. The project manager does a fantastic job explaining why it's Red but it needs to stop going Red in the first place. Identify the circumstances that would invoke each of a Red, Amber or Green Status and build warning systems around each of them. Track them daily on the JFDI project at a morning 15-minute stand-up session with the team.

- Ensure effective communication is encouraged and people are thanked for raising issues that need to be addressed by management, as soon as they occur.

- Finally, make sure you have the necessary executive commitment in all customer and supplier organisations. There will be times when unpleasant decisions may have to be made and you need to ensure management have the data to make them. It is absolutely acceptable to take resources, both system and people, away from lower priority projects to keep the JFDI firing on all six cylinders. Tough as this may sound it's either a JFDI or it isn't. Make your mind up everybody and do whatever is necessary.

The good news is that if you can manage a JFDI project and deliver to everyone's expectations then you can probably manage anything. Why not be a real hero and document a method that works for every single JFDI project. Please bear in mind though that your senior management have an absolute responsibility to explain to business executives that the JFDI card should only be used sparingly. It is not a sustainable way of working as everyone would become burned out very quickly if it was.

At the very least though, there will be some valuable lessons learned, good and bad, so ensure these are communicated and available to the entire organisation and its customers. I guarantee that you will have discovered ways of working that are applicable to every project and will add value to what you do, so make sure the word gets out.

## JUNK I.T.

**Q:** I went on holiday for 2 weeks last month and I came back to 300+ internal e-mails. Fortunately my company does work in the security sector so we are not allowed to receive external e-mails otherwise it would have been much worse. Is it the same everywhere?

**A:** Are we struggling for questions in the J category? This looks as dull as ditchwater.

Junk mail is pervasive and I think it's degenerated considerably in recent times. People have forgotten how to use their mouths on work-related topics. In a recent assignment, an individual sitting next to me would jabber on all day about personal issues or the price of fish but when it came to a work related matter, an e-mail would be sent. I found this infuriating and told them so even though they had nothing to do with me. If this behaviour is multiplied across a large organisation, then the cost of running an e-mail service must be prohibitive and wasted effort multiplies. These people often sit together for goodness sake!

We have rules and regulations, standards and policies, dos and don'ts on the most ridiculous things such as 'Don't pour coffee in the cold water dispenser' or 'Don't misuse the plant pot' but a few obvious rules around e-mail etiquette are avoided like the plague.

I once sent a 2mb file to 20 people after a monthly meeting and one of the operations guys gave me a right ticking off about abuse of e-mail and the network as it is just as easy to store it once and send everybody the link to the stored document. He was absolutely right to do so. I hate links but the point is that my personal preferences are not as important as efficient communication and the most effective use of the company's infrastructure.

The other thing that really annoys me is if I get copied in on an e-mail, sometimes with a massive attachment or link to a library I have no access to, and the sender does not indicate why I have been copied or what they want me to do. Talk about covering one's backside.

It's simply too convenient to footnote a comment to a valid problem e-mail, send it to 20 people and it then immediately becomes someone else's problem to resolve. We may never know who! And don't you just love it when you get copied in for the first time on an e-mail chain that has been running for days and there are 20 previous messages of gibberish to wade through!

I think it is the same everywhere; we need to think about it a bit more and stop wasting time!

Let's hope for a more interesting set of questions soon. Next up, the advantages of gloss paint over emulsion and why train timetables are growing in popularity.

# JOYBRINGERS

**Q:** I have just listened to a 45-minute presentation about why it is management's responsibility to create harmony and joy in the workplace. I'm convinced I dreamt it but is this such a crazy idea and too much to ask?

**A:** I bet you thought joy in the workplace was one of the canteen ladies before you went along to the presentation? I think the words are somewhat cringe-worthy but I totally support the sentiment.

It is management's responsibility to create a positive environment where excellent work can get done and people are properly rewarded for doing it. It's not management's job to do the 1,001 other things that they currently do all day that generally get in the way of progress. I've always worked on the inverted pyramid approach where I am there for the team. I find it creates a better atmosphere, a more professional environment, people feel trusted and better results are produced. People know that I am not going to threaten them if things start going pear-shaped but sit down with them and work out a solution to bring things back on track.

I am one of the naïve few that believe I was promoted due to my ability to get things done and my experience as opposed to my ability to shout, scream and do everything myself. For one thing, I don't have the ability nor should I have.

It may well be a very positive step to give every manager a performance-related objective to create a positive working environment. The delivery of the objective could only be effectively measured via feedback from the team so why not review their comments at the end of every project. I'd love it personally and would definitely be a better manager as a result of this type of feedback.

I don't believe that joy in the workplace is a Utopian ideal and a few simple actions by management could guarantee its successful adoption as a strategy. How about :-

- All managers agree that their job is to create a positive working environment where excellent work gets done, without fear and without blame.
- Relinquish command and control. Empower and trust teams or individuals but be prepared to take a bullet for them if necessary.

94

- Actively demonstrate that you think the quality of the team's work is important.
- Always celebrate a successful outcome – even a simple thank you goes a long way. An exotic holiday goes that much further of course!
- Lead – make sure your people work on the right things.
- Manage – make sure your people do the right things right!
- Be available, be approachable and bring the teas and coffees in if it's your turn.
- Join your team at lunch – don't always sit with your peers or the grown-ups.
- Always demonstrate the company values as you are the role model.
- Listen to your team and share good practice. Knowledge is not power so don't set your watch back 20 years. Things will only get worse.
- Enjoy your work and have a good time but always make sure professionalism is never ever compromised.
- Keep an eye on the stress levels within your team and always have a quiet word if you're concerned. Don't exacerbate the situation by threats or shouting. Make sure the work / life balance makes sense.

# JUSTIFYING THE REASON TO BELIEVE

**Q:** Due to lack of interest and lobbying by a couple of senior managers, the improvement programme that I launched 3 months ago has had its headcount reduced by 50% while I work on a justification. I don't think it's my job to do it, do you?

**A:** In cloud-cuckoo land, where everyone lives happily ever after, where there are fairies at the bottom of the garden and your manager says thank you when you do a good piece of work, I would agree. However, back in the jungle, if you don't do it then nobody else will. This may seem somewhat illogical to a lot of people as: -

1. You didn't personally launch the initiative.
2. You have limited authority.
3. You have severely limited or no budget.
4. You have limited line management responsibility
5. You have a problem.

It is painfully obvious that you work for an organisation where there is no real leadership. This is quite common. I've spoken to a number of people who work in Quality Assurance or Project Management Offices or Improvement Teams. They nearly all tell me that they continually have to fight for the right to exist, struggle like crazy to get things done in a better way as well as continually gaining and regaining senior management commitment to their initiatives.

This may sound ludicrous but it really is common practice. I will somewhat rascally propose that it is the only repeatable process a lot of places have. Can you imagine someone who knows nothing at all about the I.T. industry coming in one day and finding this out for the first time? They'd dine out on the story for a year. 'Guys, did you hear the one about the I.T. Director who gave one of his people half a million quid to make things better and then asked for a justification a few weeks later?'

Let's get one thing absolutely clear. The return on investment proposition for any type of improvement initiative is not calculable when you start off. Sure, there's loads of industry data but this is only available from organisations that have actually done it or at least had a go at it. They didn't have the data when they started so it took a leap of faith, an intuition, a gut feel, the sort of things possessed by leaders.

So please don't try and justify your raison d'etre with someone else's figures as the audience will glaze over and lose the will to live. Forget posters as they tend to alienate. Try it from a 'benefits / value to the customer' perspective. For example 'we need to dramatically improve the way we develop and manage our requirements or our offshore benefits case will fly south along with the millions we plan to save'.

That should wake some people up. They may be reading the paper, picking their nose, looking out the window or scratching their backside, but they'll hear that loud and clear. Paper will fly everywhere, the air will turn blue and the management team will be a dangerous place to be for a while. However in order not to alienate them totally, give them a get out of jail free card. A couple of slides on 'how to sponsor improvement' may go down well.

However, if you're stuck then here are a few ideas that should generate some healthy debate, raised eyebrows and filthy looks.

## THE TEN COMMANDMENTS FOR IMPROVEMENT

| | |
|---|---|
| 1 | Thou shalt insert improvement into everyone's objectives or thou shalt not pass Go and not collect any pay rises or bonuses. Thou will however collect a sharp object that will be metaphorically inserted where the sun shineth not |
| 2 | Thou shalt take personal and collective responsibility for the activities of the improvement programme |
| 3 | Thou shalt provide funds from your existing budgets by working differently |
| 4 | Thou shalt prioritise this programme along with all other internal changes we are doing to make sure we can deliver a realistic plan and avoid change overload |
| 5 | Thou shalt provide your best resources to help out when needed |
| 6 | Thou shalt communicate to your people as to why this is so bloody important |
| 7 | Thou shalt walk the talk – thou shalt not talk the talk |
| 8 | Thou shalt reward excellent work and convert the fire-fighters |
| 9 | Thou shalt report progress to me on a weekly basis with a dashboard etched from molten lava |
| 10 | Thou shalt remove the nay-sayers from our organisation – now go forth and multiply and get on with it! |

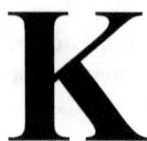

# K

*'To be conscious that you are ignorant is a great step to **Knowledge**'* – *Benjamin Disraeli*

## KAY'S CORNUCOPIA

It's now time for a quick change in format mainly due to the fact that I have failed to uncover any decent questions starting with the letter K. Well none of any interest to me and it is after all my show. So I've given myself a good stiff talking to and have deliberated on the following possibilities: -

- **Knowledge** – pretty obvious as we work in a knowledge industry. I suppose I could have written a meaty tome about the importance of knowledge transfer but that would bore both of us to death.

- The **KISS** principle – Keep it Simple Stupid. Well big deal, the I.T. projects of today aren't simple. I may have been able to fill up a page about keeping processes simple but the average guy on the street should know that this is the right thing to do. However it is worth noting for the rocket surgeons amongst you that not everything can be documented on one side of A4. An explanation of how nuclear fission works deserves a more measured approach. Perhaps a better way is to tailor the explanation or description to the most appropriate size. Don't over-engineer is the key message otherwise you will lose your audience as I'm probably doing right now. So I'll shut up.

- **Kamikaze** – no not suicide pilots. It actually means divine wind but I've spoken enough hot air in this book so far and it's a bit repetitive to keep on about Death Marches and the like. I'll take this no further.

- **Kill** – bad word but I'd be talking about projects that should be drowned at birth and not actually killing anybody. Although I'm not the homicidal type, there have been a number of people whose careers I'd like to have killed. Again, no place in a book of this gentle persuasion.

So enough of this nonsense, I'm going to write about Key Performance Indicators (KPIs), pronounced Kay-Pee-Eyes. I'm sure I used to date someone with that name.

The following are not any old KPIs even though my spell checker tried to change it to KIP just now. How very Freudian! Oh no, these are proper KPIs with crash helmets, bullet-proof vests and a large helping of pragmatism. They may not be recognisable in your organisation but they may be of some use to you.

These KPIs apply to probably the best I.T. Company in the world and the cynics amongst you will say these are not real KPIs because they don't mention employer of choice once. Well that is deliberate as a real employer of choice will focus on being excellent in delivering better value for its stakeholders and not messing about with nebulous arty-farty, touchy-feely and immeasurable mumbo-jumbo.

So why do people join companies? Look at me rambling again. I hope it is to work with the best; not necessarily to be the best paid but certainly the best rewarded. I remember talking complete nonsense in a bar a few years back, as was my wont in those best forgotten days, when some bean counter interrupted my flow and told me that people leave companies first and foremost because they have no respect for their manager. Interestingly salary was in about seventh place. I do hate having my flow interrupted but it was a point well made.

Let's imagine that we are blessed with a green field company that has just been established. It has an amount of external investment and I've managed to beg, steal or borrow some facilities, equipment and resources.

So what should the mission statement be in its first year purely from a KPI perspective?

How about the following strap-line?

**THERE WILL BE NO KPIs IN YEAR 1 – THERE WILL NEVER EVER BE A MISSION STATEMENT**

I added the last bit about mission statements because I think they are usually a ridiculous waste of time, generally all the same and usually involve lots of brown bag lunches and posters. You go home on a Friday evening and by Monday morning the office walls are covered with pictures of lions and tigers. Not only that but a dozen so-called communication champions have emerged over the weekend from beneath the skirting boards.

So what on earth will we do in Year 1 without being hypnotised by the ubiquitous KPIs? I know it's tough to lose these valued friends but the world will continue and life will still be worth living, even if it's in a KPI-less state!

This is what we are going to do. We will establish a DNA for our new company that will take a maximum of 12 months to create. Some data will be collected, no idea what yet but what is certain is that at the end of the first year we will have a clue as to where we are.

Once we've delivered a few things, customer satisfaction scores will be derived by talking to them. This may not work but let's live a little and give it a go. Once we've recruited a few people, employee satisfaction will be derived by talking to them as well, individually and collectively. We'll get ideas from the people doing the work, a revolutionary approach.

From Day 1 of Year 2 we will have our KPIs back, accompanied, no doubt, by a huge sigh of relief from the concerned masses. I'm only going to buy into this as we will have a year's worth of data, rabidly analysed by Metricsman, so our benchmark is set and our targets can then be published for the first time for all to see, especially our customers.

There will be 5 and 5 only; maybe 6 at a push but no more than 6; definitely not 7.

The all important KPIs would look something like this: -

1. **Sales** – Yep – we'd like some. The goal is to break even by the end of Year 2, which will mean any start-up losses incurred in Year 1 will need to be made good in Year 2.
2. **Delivery Precision** – improve the number of projects delivered on time to our customers by 10% from the Year 1 benchmark data. Simple measure but will be challenging.
3. **Quality** – increase the number of defects removed before System Test by 20% over Year 1; decrease the number of

100

defects found in System Test by 10%; decrease the number of defects found by the customer by 30%.

4. **Cost** – reduce the annual cost of support by 15% from Year 1; increase the amount of development work by the same amount i.e. same headcount – more new work – increased productivity – deep joy.

5. **Customer Satisfaction** – having simply spoken to them in Year 1, explain the goals for Year 2 and if we really must, send them a survey at the end of month 6 and again at the end of month 12. Strive to attain a 10% improvement between M6 and M12, but don't stop talking to them. Remember that good news and bad news are of equal value and we won't get thanked for hiding bad news until the 11$^{th}$ hour.

6. **Employee Satisfaction** – having communicated with them effectively in Year 1 by talking to them, ask them to forward just one idea that they would like to see implemented in Year 2 and why. Ensure follow up by getting a group of people nominated by the people for the people to prioritise these, no more than 3 at a time, and present a rolling 3-month improvement plan to the entire company. Take down any residual posters and mug shots and replace with these targets instead.

There will be a lot more detail to underpin these less than 7 KPIs but from an executive perspective, a summary is all that is of interest. Management can then put on their strategic hats and start working out where to go in Year 3. There will be no blue sky thinking or pontificating about where we will be 5 years down the road as that's just stupid in today's financial turmoil or at any time come to think of it.

Oh and I'd like a plasma screen in my office that simply has this dashboard – Less than 7 squares, Less than 7 colours – all Green would be kind of nice so I can change channels and watch the cricket in peace!

# L

'*A sense of humour is part of the art of* **Leadership,** *of getting along with people, of getting things done – Dwight D. Eisenhower*

## LEADERSHIP MAINLY - WITH A SOUPCON OF OTHER BITS AND BOBS

Unlike the previous chapter, there are a number of questions that qualify for the 'L' category and I touch on these briefly below. However there is one fundamental topic that on its own, can make or break an organisation, whether it's technology driven or not – and that is Leadership.

Without outstanding leaders, even great managers cannot be effective. As Peter Drucker observed 'Management is doing things right; leadership is doing the right things.' This explains, quite succinctly, the chasm of difference between management and leadership. Without exceptional leadership, managers and teams get dragged into activities akin to rearranging the deckchairs on the Titanic. There's no point being efficient if the ship is holed below the waterline.

Before we touch on leadership, there are two other questions that I feel are worthy of inclusion.

Firstly, someone wants to know the value of Lessons Learned as part of the closedown phase of a project. Is it worth it just because it is recommended in a project management methodology? Secondly, another wants to know if lifecycles are worth the paper they are written on.

Lessons Learned first then. No, I don't think you should document Lessons Learned just because a method says you should. All that gets you is a tick in the box from Audit or Quality Assurance and what's the point in that? It would be pretty dumb and just gets us into the realms of following a recipe without really understanding what the end product will look, feel and taste like.

It is good practice to document what went well on a project and what didn't go as well as expected, but the outcomes must be treated as an asset for all and used as input to future projects. It is a good way of becoming a learning organisation. This is why it should be done and for no other reason.

Try and find someone who can design and build an easy to access solution that can be made available to everyone from their desktop and focus on capturing the big ticket items for posterity. Let's avoid stuff like the customer really liked the requirements documentation because the page numbers incremented by 1 each time a page was turned.

The other thing I would encourage you to consider is putting an additional section in the Project Initiation Document or whatever your company standard is for defining how the project will be managed. Any Lessons Learned from previous projects can be documented there and can be challenged if the section is not completed.

There may be nothing worth mentioning but at least it shows senior management, assuming they read anything useful, that you have at least considered the possibility. But don't have a Lessons Learned session if no further use is going to be made of the results. You would be wasting everybody's time, money and patience.

The second question on lifecycles is linked in a way. Lifecycles are only of use if people using them really understand why they are being used and don't just follow them blindly without giving any thought into why a particular deliverable is produced at a particular stage of the project or activities are performed in a certain order.

I've seen this happen on so many occasions. I ask people why they are producing a particular document and all they can tell me is that it says so in the book. This is maddening. It's difficult enough developing systems across the time, cost, quality and requirements spectrum without some idiot producing a delightful document that no-one is going to either review or use later in the project. Kindly desist and think about what you're doing and why you're doing it.

Generally, lifecycles contain both mandatory and optional deliverables. I like the idea of a breakdown structure based on deliverables that are applicable and fit for the project's purpose, including support teams after implementation. Each project team should have its tailored version of the organisation's lifecycle that fully exploits the technology in use and their way of working. Whether this is waterfall, iterative, spiral or whatever, bothers me not one jot. What does bother me is that the team have sat down and as a group selected the most appropriate lifecycle for the project and agreed the deliverables under a 'Less is More' banner.

In summary then, let's agree that lifecycles are a good thing but only when everyone understands how to use them.

So if it's OK with everybody, now that the starters have been cleared from the table, I'll serve the main course which is a healthy portion of leadership.

To confirm my experience one more time, Leaders and Managers are not the same thing. Leaders hum a tune and managers sing it. Managers climb up steps to paint a house whereas leaders put the steps against the right house. For me leaders are born and rarely made. They are happy to make mistakes when doing the right things but detest doing the wrong things to perfection. You can train managers to be efficient without them being leaders but you try it the other way round and apart from exceptional people, you are asking a hell of a lot.

When I think of great leaders in history, they all have one thing in common, and that's the courage of their convictions. Richard Branson would not have created Virgin if he just listened to his brain. A man would never have walked on the moon if President Kennedy had said 'OK, give it a go NASA - if you really must'.

The same applies to I.T. organisations. There are sometimes things you know instinctively have to be done. They may be invisible or impossible to build a business case around, but you go for them because you know it's the right thing to do. If you succeed you are exceptional and if you fail you get kicked. That's life!

All leaders are willing to be warriors of a common cause and put their jobs on the line for something they passionately believe is right. If they aren't then they are not leaders and nothing, not one thing, will ever change.

So staying with the I.T. theme, if you are a Chief Technology Officer or Chief Information Officer or I.T. Director or Head of I.T. then perhaps you'd be kind enough to explain the subtle differences between these roles? Is it the size of your package? Whatever it is, I would hope that you lead your troops into the Promised Land and display the following behaviours on the journey: -

✓ Lead from the front. Leave us in no doubt where we're going, why we're going there and show us what the world will look like when we get there. Tell us what's going to happen in the next couple of years and not the next couple of hours. Have a vision, a goal, a dream, and a planning horizon greater than 20 minutes.

✓ Be passionate about everything you do. We won't care if you swear, shout and scream at us as long as you do it in your office with the door shut and leave us in no doubt why it is so important, whatever it may be.

✓ Communicate Communicate Communicate. Use whatever forums you have at your disposal to get a consistent message across on a regular basis. Don't sit in your office with the door shut having meeting after meeting after meeting. People will think you are a dangerous animal that mustn't be fed with any feedback at all.

✓ If you ask for comments then listen to them. Give your views on the feedback to make sure you keep getting it and if it's a good idea then reward it and get the people whose idea it was, to implement it. If it's not going to cut the mustard then explain why. Don't be dismissive.

✓ Walk the talk. You shouldn't have to wear a bowler hat with Kiss Me Quick on the front and I'm the I.T. Director on the back. Don't forget to ask about quality as well as productivity when you're out on the shop floor. Developers strive to do outstanding work so let them know you want them to and will reward them for doing so. Please don't ever stop and ask directions to the shop floor as it's not the greatest motivational message and people will talk about you!

✓ Reward the right behaviours and ensure there are consequences in place to address the wrong ones. If you've done all you can to get your message across and it's something you passionately believe in then sadly it has to be thanks for your efforts but it's time to part company with people who consistently ignore your direction. Don't forget to thank all the heroes for their outstanding contributions in the past and that you'd very much like them on board with you for the new ways of working in the future.

✓ Tell your direct reports that the vision and values you cherish are non-negotiable. Do not tolerate covert operations or opposition when one thing is agreed in your office and then the opposite happens as soon as the meeting concludes. Insist on teamwork and spell out the actions if people don't buy in. Rid yourself of any executive stealth bombers

✓ Actively encourage and sponsor improvements and then track the work personally. Ask awkward and challenging questions when things aren't moving as quickly as you'd hoped.

✓ Encourage, Energise, Motivate and most of all have the courage to follow your instincts. Don't listen to expensive consultants who always focus on the soft targets.

# M

*'The first law of bad **Management** – if something isn't working, do more of it!' – Tom de Marco*

## FROM HERE TO MATURITY

**Q:** When working with offshore companies, we have insisted that all of their internal software organisations have achieved or certainly aspire to achieve high maturity in software and systems. I have looked at the data and notice that very few companies outside of the major off-shoring centres or the United States have formally achieved this. Is this a management, technical or cultural issue?

**A:** Assuming it is an issue, which it may not be, then from my experience I wouldn't hesitate to vote Management, Cultural and Technical, in that order. I am coming at it purely from the UK angle and only then from companies I have worked with or know a lot about.

When acquiring software from a UK supplier, I would not consider them unless part of their offer included an aspiration to improve and add real quantifiable value to the relationship. They don't have to use a particular model or attain a particular level of maturity but I would insist in sampling evidence of quality activities as well as evidence of their delivery precision and customers' comments.

How else could I be confident that I wouldn't get a defect-ridden product that would take an inordinate amount of time and effort to get through operational acceptance? On what basis could I give my customers confidence that they can plan based on my promises?

OK, I could easily negotiate penalty clauses into the engagement but that doesn't help my customer and let's face it, if you have to rely on a piece of paper then the relationship is usually irretrievably broken. You don't get a contract out to read it or put your fries in it. It's generally because you're either considering legal action or termination.

How could I be sure that they have understood my requirements and won't deliver a book when all I wanted was a case to put them in?

There is a view in some quarters of the management community that quality activities are optional, simply because they are not being beaten up by their customers for delivering a solution that needs a lot of attention after Go Live. But they are being beaten up for being late. So their choice is pretty straightforward unless of course there is a safety, security or reputational consideration.

It's natural behaviour from management and I guess if customers are happy with the costs they are getting charged for I.T. then there's little point in fixing something that isn't perceived by them as broken.

The problem will come if companies no longer get paid for fixing their own defects, such as many commercial organisations or profit centres. There may even be internal customers with a bit of common sense who decide that it is not acceptable to have so many people in support as its inflating their charges, even though only internal money transfers are involved.

So the answer is simple for me. It's a management issue but we haven't quite reached the stage that it is perceived as a problem that needs urgent attention. No-one is really hurting or feeling any pain. With a few notable exceptions, no-one's life is at risk and the bonuses continue to be paid irrespective of outcomes.

The cultural issue is a significant challenge. Human nature says that if I am being rewarded for doing what I'm doing then why should I change? There is a widely held view that software improvement models, if adopted, will stifle innovation and cost their customers much more money for very little return. There is some truth in this but only if you simply follow the models blindly or only use the models themselves and nothing else.

To change this attitude requires strong leadership and a realisation that a little bit of knowledge is a dangerous thing. I've heard senior executives state quite openly in front of an informed group that they are at maturity level 1.8 and that's good enough for them. They don't know what Levels 1-5 mean but they know what 0.8 of a level means. Aaaaarghhh!

There are rarely technical issues that preclude high maturity. As an industry, we are reasonably competent at resolving technical issues. If we weren't, it would be akin to a footballer not being able to kick a ball or pass it to someone with the same colour shirt on. Surely that would never happen?

So the usual culprits are the management and cultural issues. We've all read about huge public sector projects spiralling out of control and yet, still nothing happens and it seems to me that the same offenders are then awarded the next big deal with no consideration of past performance. After all, it's only the taxpayers' money!

Finally, I fear that a number of outsourced development organisations are striving for professional accreditation, simply to put a badge on their web-site in an attempt to win business. There is nothing wrong in this as long as the prospective customers have their eyes open and ask some challenging questions prior to making a contractual engagement. Understand what you are getting into!

## MEETINGS, MEETINGS AND MORE MEETINGS

**Q:** This is not really a question, more of an observation. I never cease to be amazed as to why there are so many meetings in my company. I can rarely get to see my manager and even when I do he is constantly being interrupted. Also on the rare occasions when I need to hold a meeting, there are never any rooms available.

**A:** This is not really an answer, more a statement of the obvious. People love meetings. They like getting into a room to talk about things. You can easily put off today's problems by organising a meeting in a week's time to discuss it and people say 'My word that guy's on the ball. We raise a massive problem today and he's already organised a meeting of 12 people for the middle of next week to address it; he'll go far'. The further the better in my opinion!

The world has gone barking mad. Key decision makers are rarely available to make key decisions and when they are they seem to want a committee involving 'The Safety in Numbers Team'.

Their day is littered with back-to-back meetings and it usually takes on the look and feel of an airline schedule. The first incoming flight is late landing and that then screws up the rest of the day. People can never catch up, so they're late for every subsequent meeting on that day which shows an incredible lack of respect for other people's time.

By the end of the day, there are mountains of e-mails to address, especially those beauties with loads of links and a few massive attachments, which are too big to send around the network during office hours so you have to wait until the network is less busy, which causes further delays in response, and on it goes.

It's a vicious circle that just causes stress for everybody and resolutions for nobody and I would suggest the following are pre-requisites to all meetings or just don't show up.

(Note: these are only relevant if you really MUST have meetings; even if these protocols are adopted, there will still be too many meetings but at least they may run a little smoother and be less tiresome).

So please ensure that the following are in place before you waste your time:-

- There is an agenda that clearly states start time, duration and location. Always a good start!
- Any pre-meeting review papers are available in advance of the meeting, not at the meeting.
- It is clear what is expected of each attendee and why they have been invited.
- There is a strong chairman so at least it's got an outside chance of starting and ending on time and keeping on-subject.
- Actions are taken and these are progress chased in between meetings.
- Back-to-Back Meetings are banned. It's the law.

The classics are the regular management get-togethers that are usually held behind closed doors every week. You know the ones. There are never any visible outcomes, no white smoke ever appears, no actions are ever taken, and so what's the point. If all the managers are meeting on a weekly basis then surely they do not just discuss confidential matters, especially as there is very little outside the borders of HR-land that is actually confidential. Surely they must be discussing things that have an impact on all of us. So why can't we get to hear about them? Why can't key decisions be published?

To be fair, I have worked in places where this is done very well and it is a rare occurrence but very refreshing when you experience it.

The scientist in me breeds an assumption that if you added up all of the hours in any one year that are spent in meetings, in any reasonably-sized company, you will probably find it's not a million miles away from the number spent on new development work. I've lost count of the times I've overheard the following conversation 'How did the meeting go?' with a response along the lines of 'Oh please don't go there. It was a total waste of time'.

So don't agonise any more. It's a design feature of corporate life so there's little that can be done other than adopt a more professional and selective approach to meetings and try and keep everyone on topic.

Please don't do what one manager did and take all the furniture out of the meeting rooms to make the meetings go quicker. This works great for daily stand-ups of 15-20 minutes. It was a total disaster for more lengthy meetings as everyone felt uncomfortable and it didn't reduce their number at all. It did however increase the number of sick days lost due to back problems.

# MISSION IMPOSSIBLE

**Q:** I am a communications champion. I have been charged with coming up with a mission statement for my I.T. organisation and it's a real honour and a privilege. I've got a small mission control room set up and we've filled up hundreds of flipcharts which are jam-packed with fantastic ideas. Before we make our final decision, I was wondering if you have any examples of great mission statements that made you feel inspired?

**A:** Yes, as a matter of fact I do. It's based on the moon-shot speech where the President of the United States set down a challenge to land a man on the moon and bring him safely back to earth. This is a true mission statement even though many people were shocked and horrified by the absence of flipcharts and presentation slides at the time.

The perfect mission statement for me is to have a mission that puts everyone who thinks mission statements are a good idea on the moon and never bring them back to earth. The desire to come up with one should surely bar you from ever being allowed to.

What's it for? Who's it for? Why won't it alienate all the people trying to do good work and wondering why vast sums of money are being spent on posters, pens, lunches, video conferences and brainstorming sessions and they can't get funding to go on a training course?

The thing that really grates with me about this stuff is that it takes on a life of its own. Are you sure you've not got better things to do? It also worries me that you seem to have easily managed to get a much sought after meeting room, and on a permanent basis, as well as attracting mission controllers who also have nothing better to do.

I'd like to say it's a great idea but I can't. If pushed on the subject I would contribute the one I use myself that I've already mentioned countless times, and that is 'I just want to be a bit better than crap!' That's my mission in life and I'll leave others to judge whether I am close to success.

**Note from Author:** I may change my mind about mission statements if anyone can come up with a good one that fails to patronise, alienate or enrage.

## BEWARE OF THE MATRIX

**Q:** My I.T. department has been transformed. Management told us it had, so it must be true. Instead of having a closely-knit team doing a mix of development and support work, we are now part of one massive enterprise resource pool. My word! We have Heads of Function, Senior Managers, Programme Managers, Project Managers, Resource Managers, Line Managers, Development Managers, Quality Managers, Delivery Managers, Work Package Managers and Professional Development Managers.

Fortunately, Janet and John still manage to find time to do some development work but not as much as they used to. This doesn't seem like a good plan to me. Can you throw any light on this matrix management nightmare?

**A:** I hope your customers are bought in to this or there will be hell to pay. I would imagine that you have probably seen a number of consultants coming and going throughout the period of your transformation to the world of the good and the true. I would also guess that nothing has been transformed although a few things may have been slightly improved.

Matrix Management is usually one outcome from their deliberations. However I do believe there is some merit in the approach, but not much. The problem with matrix management is that it needs outstanding programme and project management to be really effective.

Why? It's because the managers rarely own the resources on their teams and with complex projects, there will be a need to co-ordinate and communicate with multiple areas. This makes planning and tracking overly complex and needs a lot of experience, influencing, negotiating and gravitas from the managers on point.

The old world of shouting won't get the job done any more. If managers aren't particularly strong at influencing, then there is a real risk of failure, as things will end up being done to them and not for them. There will certainly be a period of confusion around who owns what, who produces what and who can make decisions. This is not good and tends to make the customers more than a little nervous.

I also passionately believe in teams. Building a team and keeping it together, achieving optimum performance and high morale is virtually impossible with matrix management.

Like a lot of things, it makes sense theoretically but I've never seen it work well in practice. Maybe I should get out more.

# N

'*Numbers* – *if all statisticians in the world were laid end to end, it would be a good thing*' – *Mark Twain*

## STRENGTH IN NUMBERS

**Q:** My company are fanatically obsessed with numbers, whether they are derived from a reliable source or not. Although I appreciate that we need numbers to understand how things are going and what we are spending, is this obsession really a healthy one?

**A:** I don't believe that any obsession is healthy but all companies are judged based on their results. These are usually expressed in numbers. Shareholders would not behave in a rational manner if dividends were paid in retail vouchers. However everything in moderation is a sensible compromise.

From an I.T. perspective, numbers are critical as technology budgets reflect one of the major expenditures and executives need to know whether they are getting value for money. It's paramount that everyone understands how the numbers are derived and presented. For example, if a company announces that it wants to spend £20M on new features in the next financial year, how should this goal be interpreted by all the stakeholders?
-
- Does it mean £20M in total on new features? Is the board expecting £20M to cover every additional cost incurred as a result of these or is it expecting the full amount on the new functionality with any additional support or infrastructure costs being funded from savings to existing budgets.
- Irrespective of the answer, is it known how much it costs to produce a feature and whether the portfolio of projects can be delivered for this amount? If feature cost is unknown, then there is a high risk that the portfolio is not doable.

116

- What assurance is there that funds are targeted on the areas that will deliver the greatest business value? It's imperative to get the priorities right and ensure that the business cases stack up and continue to do so, as economic conditions change or requests for additional functionality creep in.

These are numbers that may well justify an obsession or certainly an almost rabid focus by the board. The grown ups need to really understand these figures in order to run their organisation effectively, cut out any waste and make sure their highest priority projects are on target to deliver their benefits and not starved of resources.

I.T. organisations must be driven by the needs and priorities of their customers. All too often I have witnessed low priority projects being allowed to continually flounder and consume huge amounts of time and money due to ineffective prioritisation, weak leadership and the inability to cancel projects that don't meet the financial criteria established when the initiative was launched.

I.T. has a clear accountability to its stakeholders to deliver transparent management information, including numbers, as to how their projects are progressing. There are four major questions that need to be answered on every single project: -

1. Elapsed time – where are we compared to where we planned to be at this moment in time?
2. Costs – how much have we spent compared to what we had planned to spend at this moment in time?
3. Scope – how many features have we built in comparison to the number we had planned to have built at this moment in time?
4. Quality – how many defects have we found and how many reviews have we completed compared with the number we had planned to have completed at this moment in time?

A review of these numbers can then form a major part of the Project Board agenda supported by a simple picture of the 4 quadrants showing Time, Cost, Scope and Quality, each with their own set of rules for determining Red, Amber or Green status. This output can then be discussed with the sponsor and any corrective actions agreed and assigned.

Obviously this is a very simple picture but it's a good starting point for those organisations that have nothing. Complexity can come in later if it really has to, once everyone is used to producing these vital few and simple numbers on a regular basis.

At the end of a project, a valuable set of historical data will then be available for further analysis and not just as input to the benefits tracking that will kick-in once the new solution has been running for a while. An added bonus is the contribution to the organisation-wide build up of historical data for future use on estimating new projects and improving delivery precision and quality.

Used effectively, there definitely is strength in numbers.

## NOUVEAU CUISINE

**Q:** We are being encouraged to be innovative and look at new ways of working. To date we have considered agile methods, the introduction of improved processes and industry-strength tools for configuration management and requirements analysis. What's your view on these as areas of attack and is there anything else we should be looking at?

**A:** I wouldn't have thought so! That looks like enough to be getting on with for the next few days at least but hopefully you are doing more than just considering things. The major issue I have with your question is that it doesn't explain why you are proposing to do all of this stuff? Are your real everyday problems being addressed? Why are you being asked to innovate and do things differently and what do your customers think of what you are doing for them?

I'm not sure that I'm fully wedded to anything that has a label, assuming doing things differently is one, as it often leads to the wrong sort of behaviour. What starts off as a great idea ends up submerged under the weight of a new cottage industry populated by masters, black belts and assessors. Somehow the message gets lost and nothing much changes apart from increased expenditure.

However, as long as everybody really understands what it's all about, what their roles and responsibilities are and what the desired outcome is, then you should be off to a flier. Agile anything makes complete sense to me, especially when the requirements are not very well understood up front. Any method that encourages outstanding work for customers and engages with them throughout the project has to be a better way of working.

Improved processes are great as long as it's not just the processes that are being improved. There must be a tangible benefit in the outcomes for all stakeholders. Most software process improvement projects I have worked with have failed spectacularly. Perhaps I am the common denominator but a lot is to do with stakeholders not being communicated with effectively and just changing the process and nothing else.

Tools are great. Well, great that is until the much anticipated silver bullet doesn't quite live up to what it says on the packaging. Just make sure you know what you are doing and everything will be fine, I'm sure!

Ensure everything that you do is of direct measurable benefit and not just to satisfy a lifecycle, a method or a model. Business needs are paramount and take precedence over everything else. As far as a software organisation is concerned, I will be amazed if your business customers have any desires over and above getting things done cheaper, quicker and with fewer defects. Align your improvements around these three things and you won't be far off the mark.

## NOSEBLEEDS AND OXYGEN MASKS

**Q:** I work in a very crowded office that is jam-packed with development teams. We have very little desk space or natural light but are expected to do excellent work. Senior management never visit us, in fact there are quite a few of us who wouldn't recognise any of them, even if they bit us on the legs. Have you experienced anything like this? I don't feel valued at all.

**A:** It does sound quite extraordinary but not uncommon. Lack of management visibility was very much an encouraged behaviour in the late 20$^{th}$ century. It had no place then and it certainly has no place now. I can certainly guarantee when you will receive a visit though. That's when things have gone horribly wrong, such as a critical production failure or a very late project. This is a direct result of management phones continually in meltdown with calls from irate customers wondering what the hell is going on and when their service will be restored or much-promised new system delivered.

You will undoubtedly be asked all sorts of searching, helpful questions and well thought through comments such as 'Why did it go wrong?' or 'When will the system be fixed?' or 'The I.T. Director will want heads to roll for this!' It's quite a fascinating spectator sport as people working hard to fix the problem are then confronted by an irate senior manager that they don't even recognise. In rare cases, the trip from the air-conditioned mezzanine floor to the top floor of the office has been so traumatising for the senior executives that they need oxygen masks and treatment for nosebleeds as they reach the dizzy heights of delivery or the shadowy depths of the coalface.

I'm not convinced this is common practice these days. Over the last decade, senior managers have generally sat with the teams in an open-plan office and it's probably gone too far the other way. They can't get a meeting room when they need one for a confidential meeting and probably show their faces too much as they've now been trained in management by walking about and talking alot; a little akin to election time when it's all smiles and baby hugging.

I'm sure some feel very uncomfortable with this new culture of openness or 'glasnost' and pine for the days when they used to sit in their air-conditioned offices with deep-pile carpets and large pictures. Those heady times when their PA's would visit them, ooh maybe once a day to see if they wanted anything done and maybe as little as once an hour with freshly brewed coffee and biscuits. Happy days!

My favourite story involves one particular executive who gained the respect of all of the teams by actually finding out where they sat. This was quite an achievement given that his office was on the other side of town. He actually stood up in front of everybody and said 'My door is always open. If you're over then please pop in for a chat!' Wow! This was something new; a breath of fresh air.

The trouble was, given that his office was on the other side of town and the only authorised method of getting there was by public transport at lunchtime, his door was in fact always open. Sadly, there was an absence of executive!

## WHY DO I NEED TO NEGOTIATE ANYTHING?

**Q:** At a recent personal development session with my manager, a training need was identified, by my manager of course, that I would benefit from formal coaching sessions and training in negotiating skills. I have no idea what this is going to add to my armoury as I develop software and don't negotiate the release of hostages. Can you enlighten me?

**A:** Yes I can do but I'm a little surprised that you need enlightening given that you have just had a career-based discussion with your manager. Did he or she not explain why it is important for you? Didn't you ask?

OK it matters not. Historically, possessing strong inter-personal skills has not been a major pre-requisite for software developers. In fact it has been actively discouraged with many developers not being allowed to discuss anything with their customers or in some cases never allowed to go anywhere near them at all. This had nothing to do with them having interesting skin complaints or contagious diseases either.

However, in today's world of iterative development where developers and customers are often co-located, it is absolutely critical that these softer skills are given a much higher focus. It is not really practical to have a situation where both customer and developer work jointly to develop a solution, via an evolutionary prototype for example, and when the customer asks for a change or makes a suggestion, the developer simply grunts, makes the change like an automaton and stares back at the customer in contempt.

This joint way of working delivers great results if there is a professional level of interaction, so to acquire influencing and negotiating skills will add significant value to your contribution.

It's not only in this type of environment that these skills will come in useful. There will be many occasions where you will need to influence an outcome. For example, when in meetings or in estimating sessions with your manager and customer, it is good to contribute; maybe even working with the resource managers to make sure you get to work on the projects that both challenge you and give you the work you need to develop your skills.

So my strong recommendation is that you embrace the opportunity you are being given, even though you don't quite get it yet and view these softer skills with equal importance to the technical skills in which you no doubt already excel. Always remember that it's not just what you do, it's the way you go about doing it that really creates an impression.

Just a thought!

# O

*'For myself I am an __Optimist__ – it does not seem to be much use being anything else' – Winston Spencer Churchill*

## OLD HABITS DIE HARD – OLD HATS DIE HARDER

**Q:** My manager has told everybody that we must sweep all old ways of working under the carpet and introduce contemporary methods that are more in keeping with the modern world. Can you give me some insight as to what you think he may mean by getting rid of old hat? He has put a newsletter on our company intranet but not everybody understands what he means or whether he has a carpet and most can't even be bothered to read his message.

**A:** I sometimes despair that we have lost the ability to communicate. If it's that important to him then the very least you should expect is an explanation of what he means by old ways and give you the opportunity to challenge and question. What he thinks of as old hat may well be working very well and unless an interactive dialogue is opened up then he may not be aware that he is potentially throwing the baby out with the bath water.

What I will do is offer an insight into what I have seen change for the better over my career in I.T. Some of this may be somewhat repetitive from previous questions but I think it's important to crystallise all of these points in one place.

I have witnessed a dramatic improvement in the way many senior managers interact with their people despite the somewhat extreme examples to the contrary that I have mentioned in this book. They are extreme cases but they do make a good war story on a damp autumn evening when there's nothing better to do. To be fair though I haven't really given enough praise to the organisations and managers that have made great strides forward in this area and I wanted to put that straight.

My interpretation of old hat is as follows: -

125

Old hat is senior management sitting in an ivory tower and never talking to their people. In some cases the pendulum may have swung too far in the opposite direction and there are too many communication sessions, managers' lunches and employee satisfaction surveys. No matter how trying this may seem, at least they are making an effort and the very least you can do is engage with them and let them know what you like and what you don't like. You may not like all the answers but at the very least you should expect to be told if not, then why not.

Old hat is a project manager having only one project to run with. It is not necessary to attend every single meeting on their project scope or perform a number of technical activities themselves. The team must share these activities and good practice encourages more self-management by the team, leaving the project manager to support them, solve the problems that they can't and work closely with the stakeholders. In this way more than one project can be managed at the same time making project managers more valuable and efficient.

Old hat is a development process that requires strict adherence to a one-size-fits-all method or lifecycle. Customers can and should be engaged on a virtually full time basis throughout the project and it is their responsibility to ensure their needs are delivered. It is unnecessary to have long protracted phases of development with no customer engagement whatsoever. If this happens then there is a massive risk that when the solution is built and delivered, it will not be what is wanted.

As an aside, it has always puzzled me why some customers seem content to await acceptance test as their next port of call after requirements have been agreed. If I was that soldier I'd be amazed if my requirements were interpreted exactly as I had specified them. So given that in this case I would be the sponsor's representative or proxy on the project then I would expect a right royal ticking-off if I let this happen. Making your I.T. department look bad may satisfy some egos but it won't deliver any value. There must be clear lines of communication and regular reviews between customers and developers.

Old hats are large transformation and improvement programmes that cost too much in terms of money and resource and struggle to deliver sustainable benefits. Don't get me wrong, if something is not working then it must be fixed – don't carry on doing more of the same.

If someone has a good practical idea that hasn't been thought of then they should be encouraged to implement it and share in the rewards of its success. However, please focus on small, incremental changes that have a big impact on delivery, quality and morale. Little and often is the key to success. The human capacity for change, and I can only speak for myself, is in no way matched with the amount of change going on generally and my little brain can only absorb so much. In fact, to continue my day job in an effective way, I can really only handle a finite amount of change. Surely it must be better to take longer to deliver everything than bite off too much in one go and end up with another car crash.

Old hat is the rigid compliance to a change control process that is there purely to protect against blame or fear of something going wrong. The massive advantage of agile thinking is the way it encourages change. This doesn't mean that it is not controlled as in a time-boxed world, if you add something in then you must take something out of equal value to keep the scales balanced. I would defy anyone to specify requirements with guaranteed accuracy without having sight of the developer's interpretation of them. This is why re-work is so prevalent when testing starts in earnest in a waterfall environment and this can't be good. OK waterfalls work much better if all requirements are known up front, for example a regulatory change, but that's about it.

I would encourage anybody to investigate what percentage of their portfolio falls into the requirements known at the start camp and then compare it to the percentage of projects that use a waterfall method. If it's not comparable then it is almost certain that fit for purpose methods and efficient practices have left the building.

And finally, having broken many golden rules by starting a paragraph with 'And', old hat is using testing as the only means of finding and removing defects from your products. It is irrelevant what method you are using, but reviewing key deliverables, as a peer group of informed people, and using a tried and tested process to remove defects will save you significant money and time. Yes, I know the record is stuck but I will keep banging on about this until more people get it.

I can't even begin to explain how many times I've heard people say 'We used to do product reviews but they took too long and were ineffective'. I don't believe that at all. How can anybody allow them to be ineffective? I will bet a lot of money that it's not the reviews that were ineffective but planning them in and sticking to the schedule and process are more likely to be the culprits. Why would anyone not insist on getting all of the nonsense out of the deliverables as soon as possible?

Don't even try and answer that!

## ORGANISATIONAL NIRVANA

**Q:** I work for a very large multi-national with nearly a thousand people in I.T. alone. If you look at our organisation chart, it resembles a complex grid with many layers of management to underpin it. As you've been round the block a few times, can you enlighten us as to the model that has worked best for you and your customers?

**A:** This is a no brainer! Without hesitation, it's a small outsourcing company that I worked in that was part of a much larger professional services company. I imagine one's first reaction is going to be that small is great and much easier to implement a flatter structure in and I would absolutely agree.

However, one could take a view that it is possible, with some lateral thinking, to slice and dice a large organisation into many smaller ones. As long as there is a lead in each and the communication channels are effective then anything is possible. One approach may be to chunk the work up into products or services complemented by one of the chunks being dedicated exclusively for gluing everything together.

Before I explain how the model was established, it is important to state quite categorically that I personally did not create it. It was already in place when I joined the company in question and although I tweaked it a little, the credit for its establishment rests elsewhere.

I should also point out that the outsourced software company was geared to act as an exemplar of how to perform high maturity software engineering in order to win business for the parent services company. In other words, inviting suspects and prospects to a good place and walking the talk. OK, so enough waffle!

The big selling points for me and a number of new recruits who joined us during my stay, was the total lack of any hierarchy or organisation chart and the positive move to encourage self-directing teams. As its head, I was only required to intervene operationally in any staff issues or salary decisions and even then, on the rare occasion that I had to invoke a meeting, I was joined by two members of the engineering team that were elected by the members to ensure fair play.

So how was the work allocated? As a profit centre we couldn't afford too many non-chargeable hours so we established a team of engineers to assign members to projects and tasks. They knew each other's strengths and weaknesses and where a challenge was needed. They were far better placed to allocate the work rather than an administrative resource management function. They met weekly and its membership was rotated on a regular basis. All newly created positions were advertised and all applications were then reviewed at the weekly meeting.

What did we do to ensure consistency across all of our projects and learn from good practice? This was the responsibility of the project managers to work together as a group and disseminate the learning on the next set of projects. They were supported by an excellent Quality Manager.

We also had a continuous improvement project to act on initiatives that required a little more investment prior to rollout. The project managers also reviewed progress across all projects and worked as a team to ensure we were successful in everything that we committed to. They were hard taskmasters but we never missed a delivery or quality target.

Cynics may cry 'Well that's all well and good but how did you fix any infrastructure issues, building issues or perform administrative tasks such as Expenses or Payroll?' We had yet another self-directing team, ably supported by a Group Financial Controller. These guys performed all the services you would expect to receive if you visited a 5-star hotel. This included resolving network issues, acquiring more kit when we needed it, ensuring we only used licenced software and interfacing with external suppliers for non-core services such as payroll.

When the teams decided it was time to move the office six inches to the left then this was accommodated. There was a real sense of pride and ownership and the vast majority of interior design was carried out by volunteers.

One other area deserves a special mention. We were fortunate enough to have an expert in software measurement as a full-time employee who had a vast reservoir of data on our previous projects. This enabled us to predict many outcomes in terms of defects expected in test based on the removal rate success in previous reviews as well as guaranteeing that our delivery commitments were not compromised. This provided a firm foundation for accurate estimating and enabled us to offer fixed price contracts to customers from a position of strength. The cunning plan was to re-invest

130

any profits for marketing, team building events or training but sadly profits were gobbled up by Group to subsidise under-performing units.

Two more functions to tell you about and that's it. How did we attract new business? To be honest, most of our work came to us via existing customers and it was very difficult for the Board to come to a decision to spread our wings a little wider while these cash cows were grazing very lucratively in lush pastures. We had too many eggs in one basket though. We created a small team of former project managers and engineers with strong inter-personal skills who strove manfully to win new business but at the time it was a cash-strapped market with a recession looming.

I strongly believe to this day, that if we were given more support then we could have done much better and maybe still be a thriving business. However it was not to be but I still maintain our approach was the right way to go. Maybe if I had attracted an experienced hunter to get the leads then we would have stood a greater chance of success. I regret that I did not do more to make this happen.

Last but by no means least, we have the coaches. This was our way of ensuring that our members received the professional development they needed and their technical and inter-personal needs were fulfilled. Again, quite astutely in my view, the company did not assume that managers make good coaches. Quite the opposite as we offered coaching as an optional service at peer level to help people attain their goals. It was not there to ensure people met their delivery objectives or to influence any salary review as that simply would not have worked. Coaches were volunteers who were professionally trained via a significant investment by the company and in my view, it was expertly executed.

So that's about it for the organisational model. Communication was simple and delivered weekly with the obligatory tea and cakes. I would make any group announcements and then we'd get an update from each area and invite new ideas as well as the usual Q&A. We had quarterly employee satisfaction surveys where we would identify areas for improvement and any gaps in our armoury.

As previously mentioned, it's results that count and if it's results that are needed then we had some very impressive ones.

Edited highlights as follows: -

- ✓ Our excellence in delivery precision and quality was rewarded by being voted No 1 design centre worldwide by our most significant customer. The people who achieved this formed the core of the new outsourced unit.
- ✓ Defect density of between 0.06 and 0.02 defects per thousand lines of code (KLOC) at Go Live and Go Live + 6 months respectively. This is world-class engineering although not our decision to use lines of code as the quality measure I hasten to add; it was a customer requirement.
- ✓ Regular Return on Revenue of 30%. The most profitable area in the group by a country mile.
- ✓ SW-CMM® Level 3 as assessed by our major customer's process improvement teams. This meant that we conformed to a world class model for both project and organisational practices. We also regularly retained our ISO 9000 certification from the British Standards Institute; great for the web-site, which was built and maintained internally as well.
- ✓ We never missed any delivery dates – not a single one!

Not bad – not bad at all. I was sad to move on and have not managed to quite reach the same high levels of job satisfaction since and will always look back with pride on what we achieved here and more importantly what the people achieved without the command and control structure that suffocates so many organisations. It restored my faith that if you empower people to work as part of self-managed teams, don't interfere too much but be there when asked for support then some astonishing outcomes will result.

At this point, the reader may wish to reflect on a time in their career when total job satisfaction was experienced or near as makes no difference. Ask yourself why you felt this way. Ask yourself why you tolerate anything less than this today. Ask why you are not having fun and delivering value to really ecstatic customers and maybe try and do something about it?

# BE CAREFUL – OVERHEADS ARE DANGEROUS AND MAY BITE

**Q:** We have just completed our bi-annual efficiency review and the consultants tell us that compared with other companies in our peer group, our management overheads are way too high. It is not clear to me what can be done and I need all the help I can get as our finance people are getting very excited. It's as if someone has poked a wasp nest with a sharp instrument. Any advice would be most welcome.

**A:** You need to find out which people and what activities are directly chargeable to customers, whether internal or external. This should be around 80% of the overall total for the function being measured. Anything less than this and you need to be wielding a big stick as you have too many people not directly contributing to cost recovery and these people are pushing your costs up to uncompetitive and inefficient levels. This may well explain the unfavourable comparisons in your report.

My experience tells me that business units will tolerate an overhead of around 20%. This overhead is most definitely not project management, where a 20% overhead is acceptable but it's not an overhead, even though I just said it was, as these activities should be explicitly stated on a project schedule and charged for. What should be challenged is a one project / one project manager scenario as this is ludicrous if the manager is managing and not doing 'stuff'. However this argument has already been made so I will not go on about it any further.

So where else can you look to save money? Firstly you need to assure yourself that every single cost that can be recovered from a project is being recovered. Look at the support groups and see if there is something they can charge for. Maybe some independent reviews, process development, knowledge transfer or new method introduction that is project-specific can be recovered if you can establish a strong case and agree it with your sponsor.

Make sure you are getting value for money from what you are being charged by other cost centres in your organisation. Areas to investigate would be Infrastructure, Operations, Quality Assurance, Finance, HR and central support teams. I'm not talking about application support or infrastructure support here, as this is a totally different animal and funded separately. I'm taking about shared services functions. It will also serve you well to look at both middle-management and senior management layers to see if there is some room for manoeuvre and maybe reduce the number of boxes on the organisation chart, but bear in mind you will be entering a war zone if you go down this road.

Once you have reviewed this, do some what-if analysis as to the short and long-term consequences of not funding some functions at existing levels. Who would suffer? What would be missed? A triage approach may well be appropriate but don't change anything that will impact your customer delivery capability without agreeing it with them first.

It's very much a thankless task. You know you should always be operating at optimum levels but it's easy to get complacent when there are much more immediate issues to be attended to, especially in profitable times. The function that was originally intended to assure project delivery with about 6 expert resources has now grown to 20, almost by stealth, is an example of this. It takes an economic downturn to really get the executives focused on getting value for money, driving down the cost base and only doing the absolute minimum to support company strategy. I wish you well.

## OUTSOURCE, INSOURCE, RIGHTSOURCE OR SOME OTHER SOURCE?

**Q:** Whilst travelling home last night on the 18.15 from London Waterloo, I read an interesting article in the London Evening Standard. Apparently, my company is going to outsource the vast majority of its I.T. support functions to a to-be named third party. Although the news was well received in the City judging by the hike in the share price, it was not well received on the 18.15 from London Waterloo as this was the first I'd heard of it. Why are they doing this now and what should I be doing to safeguard my job?

**A:** There's not much you can do to safeguard your current job if it's being outsourced. That's the point of it. However, if you can retain a positive attitude and support the initiative, irrespective of how it was communicated, then there may be some new roles in the mother ship as a direct result of the decision. This often happens when the skill needs move more to consultation and acceptance as opposed to fix on fail. Just keep an eye on announcements, hopefully not always via the media, and see what you can do to help. It may turn out to your advantage if you embrace the change.

So why do it now? Well if your company hasn't dipped its toe in the outsourcing water yet then it was only a matter of time, wasn't it? Obviously they will smell the cost saving carrot. Perhaps someone who is high up in your organisation's food chain has attended a conference and been persuaded that this is the way forward, not only from a cost perspective but also with the potential to link the initiative to service improvements.

Ultimately the decision should be based on a sound strategy. How can we maximise the value for money that we deliver to our customers? How can we improve the service? What are the competencies that we must retain and grow in our company?

Certainly outsourcing changes the landscape significantly. It will however take time to transition the support to a third party as there will be an intense period of due diligence and knowledge transfer before this can happen and you may find that you are not as much at risk as you first thought once details of the deal emerge.

There will still be a number of roles that will be required to make the outsourcing deal effective. There will need to be expert domain knowledge

135

to ensure that critical services are not compromised by the initiative. In some cases I've known financial incentives to be offered to people to hang around until the third party can stand on its own two feet. This makes perfect business sense for both parties.

Business analysis and project management skills will need to be retained, as will Configuration, Release and Change Management skills. These are normally retained as core functions and will need improvement as the acceptance activities become much more critical. There may also be a level of problem and incident management retained so customers have direct access to support staff who really understand how everything hangs together and can get things done quickly, especially during the transition. Service or Help Desk outsourcing decisions vary from organisation to organisation; some outsource but some retain them as core functions.

From experience outsourcing generally takes a little longer, costs a little more and uncovers a few more risks and issues than were originally anticipated. Generally I have seen this work very well from a support perspective. I'm in no way convinced that this is always a good idea from a new software development perspective but that's another issue. Never forget though, that as far as your customer is concerned you are still responsible for support, the major change being that it is now a managed third-party service. The risk however remains with you!

# P

*'A good __Plan__, violently executed now, is better than a perfect plan next week' – George S. Patton*

## PLANNING PERMISSION

**Q:** Are you an advocate of detailed project plans and what constitutes a good plan?

**A:** Yes I am, but not as much as I used to be. When I first started out in project management, not many people used to produce schedules let alone plans, but if you were lucky there would be the odd manager who would diligently produce a hand-drawn Gantt chart and distribute it to the team or simply pin it up on a notice board. Some would even keep it up to date and use it.

I'm not convinced that this was of great benefit other than to give the sponsor a level of confidence that the teams were being managed and that at least someone had given a little bit of thought as to what tasks were to be performed, in what order, how long they should take and who would perform them.

This somewhat light touch to planning was really only scheduling and it was superseded by a much more detailed and time-consuming approach, culminating in a document that we now know and love as the Project Plan.

The Project Plan includes a detailed breakdown of how the project is going to be approached, managed, governed and in some cases how quality is going to be built in. It would also include a detailed schedule showing a work breakdown structure of potentially hundreds of tasks before any work had even started or any resources were assigned.

Thus the planning pendulum had swung dramatically from the back of a cigarette packet sized deliverable to a monumental manuscript, which took ages to produce and more importantly became too time consuming to keep up to date or even read. Things had moved too far in the wrong direction and this begs a fundamental question. Why would anybody produce a document of such size and complexity and then not keep it up to date or use it to manage the project? However the auditors and quality assurance guys loved it but the project team rarely knew of its existence.

So yes, I am a fan of detailed plans with a huge caveat that the plan must only contain the appropriate level of detail that is just enough to govern the project effectively. It must be a living document and used by the team and not something the project manager has created for the benefit of others outside of the project.

I know there are new methods of planning being used today that involve tasks being derived by the team where they each volunteer for the work and estimate how long each task will take. The team also track progress and revise estimates on a regular basis. Surely this will only work if performed by a mature team, one that possesses expert knowledge in the technical and business domains. If it does and an environment exists that encourages this way of working then it sounds great. In my experience this is very rare and so it is usually left with the project manager to do the planning. On rare occasions the plan may even reflect the priority of the requirements and their value to the stakeholders.

To summarise then, I think plans are essential and if used effectively and produced with just enough process to get the job done then they can be great communication vehicles and a channel for letting all engaged parties know what's going on and where the pinch points are. Surely the alternative of not producing anything, with everyone arriving at work each morning and doing whatever takes their fancy cannot be viable.

It may be worthwhile considering only having a crisis plan given that most projects reach a critical point at some stage and then it's all hands on deck to drag it over the line, kicking and screaming. If this is normal procedure then the plans need to reflect this, as do the methods and lifecycles in use. I realise this sounds ridiculous but think about it for a little while and try and fit the planning approach that would have really worked on previous projects you have worked on.

So what constitutes a good plan in terms of content, apart from brevity and usability?

## Approach
It's a good idea to document how the project will progress in terms of ways of working. Will it be a traditional waterfall method or a more agile approach where early value is a significant outcome? How will Lessons Learned from previous projects be considered? Why not hold a brief definition workshop with the key players and get this agreed up front and documented.

## Governance
How will the project be governed? What steering groups will be established, why and who will attend the meetings? How will progress be reported in terms of budget and timescales? How will risks and issues be identified and tracked to closure? What independent quality assurance is necessary? How are dependencies going to be managed? What roles and responsibilities need to be agreed and documented?

## Planning & Tracking
How will the work be broken down from the requirements? Who will do what? How long will each activity take? How were the estimates derived? How will change be accommodated? How will the team know exactly where they are on the project? Do we have enough of the right resources in terms of both skills and numbers? Have we re-estimated future tasks based on the actual time taken on completed tasks to date? What metrics will we collect? It is important to remember that it's impossible to accurately breakdown the work from start to finish before any work has started, so bite off a bit at a time. This will save hundreds of hours.

## Quality
What deliverables are we going to review and what process will we use? How will we know whether the defect removal method is effective? What testing will be done and how from both a functional and non-functional perspective? Will we need independent health-checks and how many?

## Stakeholder Interfaces
Identify who needs to be engaged whether it is from the business, other I.T. teams such as support, testing or infrastructure or third party suppliers. What do they need to know and when? How are you going to implement the solution? What training or skills transfer do we need to plan and execute?

**Environmental considerations**
Do we have everything we need to build, test and go live? Are there any additional hardware or software requirements? How will we build and integrate the software as it gets developed and tested? How do we do this? What is our approach to configuration management?

**Change and Release Management**
How will change be accommodated? What process will we use? Can anybody raise a change? How will software be released, when and where? What types of release will be supported?

For me, these are the main considerations. In an ideal world you would simply cross-reference an existing process and only document any variations to keep the size of the plan down to a manageable level and also demonstrate process maturity at an organisational level.

Try as best you can to brainstorm as much as you can in workshops and time-box the production of the plan to no more than 1 or 2 days. You can always add to it or amend it later but remind yourself of the quote by General Patton at the beginning of this section and get on with things as soon as possible. Deadline dates have a nasty habit of creeping up on you and giving you the bird as they pass you by.

## PROCESS IMPROVEMENT – QUICK SUMMARY

**Q:** You may well have touched on this already but it would help me if you could point out the issues I will encounter in sustaining a process improvement programme. I have heard about many failures and too few successes. What can I do to learn from others' experience?

**A:** I'm not sure that I am the best qualified to answer your question as I have spent too much of my career working for organisations that have taken one step forward and then two steps back. Perhaps the best thing I can do is point out a few things that have worked well for me and then I'll propose some more purely based on adopting the opposite approach to that which went spectacularly wrong for me.

What follows then is a pot-pourri of my experience - good and bad. I hope this will help you to formulate your strategy and sustain a successful programme but never forget you are entering a war zone and on most occasions you will be persona non grata.

- Understand your end game. What is it that you are trying to achieve? How will you know whether a successful outcome has been achieved?

- Ensure that you fully cater for the aspirations of the senior stakeholders and those people who will be funding the work. Many people strongly advise that it is wrong to focus on a maturity level or a number and I can see where they are coming from. However, be in no doubt that the senior executives will be, as it gives them something to hang their hats on in terms of measures, as well as a benchmark to talk about with their peers in other organisations. You must bear this in mind in your strategy. It's not always about what's right from a logical perspective.

- Prepare a detailed communication strategy so that everyone understands why the improvements are necessary. Involve everybody in the preparation so that you are prioritising the work in the right way. Consider getting a brief assessment on your project management practices at least, as these are usually the ones in need of most remedial work.

- Plan to deliver improvements incrementally, in short sharp bursts. Don't bite off a huge chunk and expect to fix it all. This will take too long and guarantee failure. An agile approach will have a much better chance of success.

- Consider what data you are going to collect in order to demonstrate the progress being made, both as a baseline and on an ongoing basis. Keep this very simple to start with, especially if your organisation is not used to working in this way. Massive data collection exercises will fall into disrepute very quickly and never be of any use.

- Involve your very best performers, as they will always find the time to do that little bit extra and people will take notice. So often in the past I have witnessed behaviour that is not conducive to a successful outcome. The few change programmes that are successful should deliver a change in behaviour as well as improved customer and employee satisfaction.

- Make sure you keep everyone up to date on progress. You don't need a 25-page scorecard with coloured charts in order to do this and I would advise strongly against this. A few positive statements and a thank you or well done will do for a start. The entrees, with a little more meat on the bones, can come later once everyone is happy with the starters.

- Sustaining the improvement programme is critical to its success. You will notice very quickly that you have entered a tough neighbourhood. There will be shots fired across your bow and massive resistance to change. This is normal human behaviour; the not invented here syndrome. At the very least try and get a monthly 1:1 with your sponsor and ideally with the senior management team. Appeal to their egos and focus on their wants and needs. Ask for support at the meetings they hold with their teams. If there is one thing that I recommend above everything else is to manage all of your stakeholders and ensure their requirements are fully catered for.

- One final absolute must do. Improvement must never get in the way of fulfilling existing commitments to your customers. The process can never be more important than the outcome of a project. This is the hardest lesson and the most difficult to overcome. Communication with your customers is absolutely critical. They will only support you if they really understand that there's a big prize in it for them. Avoid comments like 'things will take a bit longer to start with', as this is not what they want to hear. They believe they are being charged too much already. Stress the benefits of doing things better in terms of overall costs, timescales and quality. If this is not acceptable then don't start the programme.

## THERE IS NO SUCH THING AS BAD PRODUCTIVITY - IS THERE?

**Q:** I have been asked by my senior management team to look into ways of improving productivity. A data collection exercise has just been completed and the results show that our productivity is average in comparison with our peer group of companies. Management have clearly indicated that they don't do average. What do you recommend?

**A:** What can I recommend based on the information you have provided? Perhaps it would be a good exercise to kidnap the management team, take them to a secret location giving them no contact whatsoever with the outside world and scream very loudly at them 'What exactly do you mean by productivity improvement? What's average? Who are the peer group? What problems are we trying to resolve?

However, that would not help much and will be somewhat career limiting for you.

Maybe the following alternative approach is worthy of consideration: -

- Establish what the productivity data is telling you, how it was calculated and how it splits out between the various activities you perform e.g. Development, Enhancement and Support. This would be a great start. Of course I do appreciate that this may involve having a conversation with a member of the measurement team. I.T's dirty work but someone has to do it. Pick straws!

- In parallel to this, have a look at what your customer feedback is telling you and if this doesn't exist, try and find a few helpful souls to give you a view. Are they dissatisfied with productivity and do they understand the difference between good and bad productivity? What is their description of productivity?

- Productivity data in isolation is absolutely useless. It needs to be put into context from a time and quality perspective. For example, if the average development productivity equates to 30 new goodies per person per month then you need to establish whether the elapsed time to deliver these is acceptable. You also need to ascertain whether the number of defects found in testing, warranty

144

and live running are at acceptable levels. If the amount of effort involved in fixing defects is disproportionately high then your test group and support teams will probably be highly productive. This is not where you need to be. This is bad productivity. If your development productivity increases to say 32 new goodies a month and the testing and support activity stays the same or reduces, then this is good productivity and the customer will almost certainly notice a difference.

- Consider other ways to improve productivity that do not solely rely on people working harder and longer hours as this has been proven to be counter productive, time and time again. Try automating the testing phases, increasing the number of deliverable reviews to drive out defects, adopting time-bound development phases and using just enough process to deliver a successful outcome. Look at industry data and identify good practice from agile ways of working and adopt as appropriate, always making sure that these are not based on a very heavy manual or textbook. Recruit if necessary!

- Have a look at the environments that your people have to work in. Are there too many interruptions? Is the feedback they need to continue with their tasks too slow in coming? Is there an unacceptable amount of noise from other groups that is distracting them from being as productive as their working environment allows?

- Are you rewarding the right behaviour? Is it productivity at any cost?

- Try and find some people in your external network that can share their experiences and then see if this applies to your organisation.

- I haven't especially focused on re-use of existing assets but this will be of tremendous value. If you re-use someone else's goodies then you gain their productivity points as well. How good is that?

- Ensure that you produce reports to evidence progress and issues, preferably on one side of A4. Ensure it is obvious to everybody how things are going and what's going to happen next. Always remember to highlight good practice as soon as it delivers benefit and encourage other teams to adopt it if it makes sense to do so.

- Keep to the 80/20 rule and implement productivity improvements little and often. It will cause you and your organisation a lot less pain.

# THE I.T. PROJECT MANAGERS' MANIFESTO

**Q:** I am an experienced project manager and have been trained in multiple Project Management Methods and certified by many industry-recognised bodies. Naively, I fully expected the job to become a bit easier as my experience and accreditations grew. What I have found though is that it has become more and more like trying to hop through quicksand. Why do you think this is and how do I become the project management guru in my company?

**A:** Wow – what a fantastic question! How good would it be if I could come up with a fantastic answer? I think I may then have the funds available to be writing my next blockbuster in somewhat warmer and more exotic climes.

Hopping through quicksand is what many projects have to go through to get close to a successful outcome. Great project managers can cut through the mire and provide a smoother passage for their teams. So how do they do it? It takes a lot of personal gravitas, courage, tenacity and experience. I've never heard of an easy project, in the same way as I've never witnessed the impact of a silver bullet.

I've not been much help so far and have probably not identified anything that you didn't know already. Mentoring and Coaching will help for sure, but not many places hold these in high esteem. So what I've come up with is a Project Management Manifesto that is a direct result of my personal failures. It contains Dos and Don'ts, Hints and Tips and what you fundamentally must not compromise on as a project manager.

If you can take some of these on board then it may not make you a guru but will certainly give you an insight into what you have to do to become, if not a guru, then a damned good storyteller for your children's children.

| THE I.T. PROJECT MANAGERS' MANIFESTO |
|---|
| Everything that is done on your project must be of quantifiable value to a stakeholder |
| Interpersonal skills, drive, teamwork, customer delivery focus and a passion for excellence are your most important attributes |
| Do everything you possibly can to deliver – don't tolerate anything that gets in the way! |
| Never let any task start if you have no idea how to finish it |

| |
|---|
| If it's not working then change it – don't do more of it! |
| Embrace but control changes. If something comes in, something has to go out OR existing commitments on time and cost need to be re-negotiated with your customer |
| Avoid any dependencies if humanly possible – these can severely damage your project health |
| Never estimate a task that you are not going to perform yourself – this won't work |
| Deliver the minimum you need to – don't worry about tomorrow's projects but always aim to beg, steal or re-use the work of others |
| Strive to create a blame-free environment where outstanding work is rewarded |
| If trouble looms, let your immediate manager know. Hide nothing. Surprise no-one! |
| Manage risks and take a few in order to deliver a successful outcome |
| Contain slippages– pretty reports documenting reasons for delay can never make up for missing dates as far as your customer is concerned |
| Never let anyone else make a decision that impacts your project without your consent or at the very least, you are given the opportunity to document any ensuing risks and issues |
| Involve the entire team in planning and tracking activities – do this very regularly |
| If you have built a great team – keep it together if you can for future projects |
| Communicate with all stakeholders – don't wait for steering groups to raise issues |
| Launch, mobilise and initiate your project in the shortest possible timeframe |
| Ensure the processes, lifecycles and methods are just enough for your project. Cut to fit. |
| Don't assume your suppliers will deliver outstanding work – validate what they do |
| Work for your team – the other way round won't work |
| Be prepared to put your job on the line for something you passionately believe is right |
| Encourage a learning organisation – publish what worked well and not so well |
| Only personally do what you personally have to do! Clear your decks daily and be available |

*'What's the use of a good **Quotation** if you can't change it'* – *Doctor Who*

## ON QUALITY STREET

**Q:** What do you think of the statement - 'Quality is Free?'

**A:** It is certainly attention-grabbing and maybe this is what its initial intention was. I don't mean my personal attention, but more to get leaders' attention on the quality problem; not just the 'when is the project going to be finished?' problem.

There is an incredible amount of nonsense spoken about quality and the perceived trade off between quality, cost and time. How on earth can you calculate the effort to be expended on quality based on time and cost? How will you know whether the effort has been effective? If someone could explain to me how this can be achieved then I would be extraordinarily grateful. Surely in order to do this you must have at your disposal a reservoir of reliable data with which you can start to do some simulation analysis and a lot of spare time to do this research; and this is in short supply.

Executing quality activities is not very hard to do. The tricky bit is trying to get all levels of management to mandate that removing defects from products is not only a mandatory cost during the development of a product but it is also exponentially cheaper than getting rid of them after the product has been built and implemented. One reason for this quality inertia could be that some key stakeholders generally only care about the cost/time equation and therefore have no interest whatsoever in what happens afterwards. Why would they? They will have moved on. So if they don't care then no-one else will.

It is a mystery why more customers don't understand the value of quality. If you can measure your quality performance and get it readily accepted that quality activities will appear regularly in the project schedule, then maybe it is free. If you can spend less time on fix-on-fail activities then more new products would get built and quality would be viewed as an imperative as opposed to a 'nice to have'.

Nobody bats a single eyelid if all the project resource is tied up on design, build and test re-work resulting from defects found too late. Why is there such an objection to trying to remove this cost forever? Only then will quality be free or if not free, understood by all.

## THIS IS MY QUEST – NO MATTER HOW HOPELESS!

**Q:** I have recently come back from a seminar where one of the speakers said that some projects are quests. I have no clue what he was talking about. Can you enlighten me?

**A:** Obviously no time for Q&A at the end of the presentation then? Maybe the lunch menu wasn't to the speaker's liking so he or she didn't hang around afterwards for an impromptu session. It seems such a basic question but here goes!

Some dictionary explanations of the word quest include: -

- The act of seeking.
- A looking for something.
- A search - as in an adventure or expedition.

So from these descriptions, the speaker may have been alluding to the characteristics of some projects inasmuch as they are so large and so complex that they can have no possible chance of sticking to any budget or timescale. Many of us have worked on these types of projects. Very few have succeeded and most fail in my experience. When Jason set off in the Argo with his Nauts in search of the Golden Fleece or Marco Polo set off in search of something that may well have ended up as China, I'm sure that their sponsors did not have any pre-conceived ideas of how much the search would cost or when, whatever it was they were looking for, would be found.

This approach cannot and must not be applied to projects. Small is good; medium is tricky; large is great to boast about in the early days and difficult to get out of when it starts to go wrong, as it inevitably will.

Everybody knows that large projects are quests and yet we still seem to have no qualms whatsoever in kicking off these poisoned chalices even though the industry data screams 'NO – IT CAN'T BE DONE!' So if you are a senior executive with a responsibility for delivering large projects, then please ensure you have the size data as well as budget and time information. Find out what the industry data is telling you on projects of equivalent size and their success rate – and then pose the odd tricky question.

If this information is not forthcoming, I suggest we all call the project a quest and pray that the Holy Grail, Atlantis, El Dorado or Mr Spock are found pretty sharpish.

I hope this was what the speaker meant. If not I make no apologies for singing the same old song as these are all points worthy of continual debate and re-emphasis. Less is more in the world of software projects.

## QUICK WIN OR SLOW DEATH?

**Q:** My employer has just appointed a senior programme director to drive in improvements and transform our I.T. department. What he has promised the executive leadership team is reduced costs and quick wins in the 'Business As Usual category? What is a quick win as it sounds as though it should be fairly obvious, especially the velocity piece.

**A:** Before I relate my experience of quick wins, I want everyone to know that I have issues with the expression Business As Usual or BAU. It implies that everything being done as BAU is good and acceptable, when patently it rarely is. 'We will sort that out in BAU' is a cry I often hear when it gets a bit tricky during the project and it makes me cringe. It's as if BAU is a place like Nirvana but in reality it's more like Cloud Cuckoo Land. If it can be sorted out in BAU then surely it can be sorted out now on the project. Don't leave it to those poor souls in BAU-land who won't have the foggiest notion of what's coming their way except that when it hits, it will hit hard.

Steve C. McConnell in his book 'Software Project Survival Guide', states that 'the problem with quick and dirty, as some people have said, is that the dirty remains long after the quick has been forgotten'. I'm sure anyone who has worked on millennium projects will understand what I'm about to say.

What started out as a quick win using say a small database or spreadsheet, now doesn't conform to any standard or perform under load. However the promised funding to upgrade it later never materialised, which isn't necessarily an issue unless anything needs to be updated, for example the minor problem of a change in millennium.

Originally, it was undoubtedly a noble attempt to achieve 'a quick win' and was so successful it became THE 'strategic' solution in the eyes of its customers. Huge amounts of critical data were then thrown at it so that it very quickly became a slow death, as it performed so badly. In many cases the next day's processing run needed to start an hour before yesterday's processing completed in order to comply with agreed availability levels, real or perceived.

An extreme example perhaps and we are talking about a systems issue and you are probably alluding to a change programme in your question.

The notion of the quick win will disappear if the change programme is planned properly. Areas that will deliver the quickest return for the lowest amount of effort should be addressed as a matter of priority. You can call these early benefits if it makes you feel better or quick wins if you simply want to cause trouble.

Whatever your choice, the trick is prioritisation with focused, short, sharp deliveries to give the programme both momentum and credibility.

**Author's Note:** There has been considerable use of the words 'transform' and 'transformation' in this book and I'm quite unclear as to what it really means in terms of results. My experience of so-called transformation programmes is not great. To me, transformation should result in an order of magnitude improvement in capability and productivity. It's an over-used word, doesn't do what it says on the tin and usually results in a huge bill and a few minor improvements if you're lucky. Generally it ends up with a few people doing more of the same, a little differently perhaps but nothing revolutionary or radical that will challenge the status quo.

# A QUOTA OF QUOTES

**Q:** I am about to give a presentation at a software conference and as it's my first one I'm a bit nervous. I thought it would be a great idea to include a few quotations to lighten the mood and get some inter-action going? Do you have any ideas or recommendations?

**A:** Yes, if you don't overdo it then it can be a terrific icebreaker. I have used quotes extensively in this book but I've done my best to attribute the quotes to their originators to avoid any litigation. I would recommend that you do exactly that, choose them carefully and make them applicable to your target audience.

Here's an example of the good and maybe not so good practices. Let's wake up my anti-acronym friend from earlier and incur some more seething anger.

Good practice if they are: -

| | |
|---|---|
| S | Specifically selected for your target audience. |
| T | Technically correct. No amendments to make them funnier. |
| U | Unbelievably funny but technically correct (see above). |
| P | Politically sensitive with no possibility to offend. |
| I | Inspirational. |
| D | Direct and relevant to the precise part of the presentation where they are included. |

Bad practice if they are: -

Connected to an acronym for good practice called S.T.U.P.I.D!

I have listed a few anonymous quotes on the next page that may be relevant to a software conference, either directly or indirectly. At the very least you won't be sued if you include them and I apologise in advance for the lack of quotation marks.

- Any simple problem can be made insoluble if enough meetings are held to discuss it.
- Why do we expect documentation to accurately describe the product when the documentation is finished first?
- We did about 10,000 tests on it and it was working fine – until Monday.
- Better train people and risk they leave than do nothing and risk they stay.
- Real programmers don't comment their code. It was hard to write so it should be hard to understand.
- Software, good software, is not built by individuals. It is built by teams. To do this, the teams must possess shared values, principles, and practices.
- If you can't beat your computer at chess, try kick-boxing.
- If you don't know how to do something, you don't know how to do it with a computer either.
- A thorough software professional is someone who, when his wife yells at him 'Go To Hell', worries more about the Go To statement than what his wife is upset about. (Note from Author: best change wife to partner to conform to the P in the S.T.U.P.I.D acronym.)
- If you don't like to unit test your product then your customers won't like testing it either.
- There are 10 kinds of people – those who understand binary and those who don't. Olden but golden!

# R

*The policy of being too cautious is the greatest **Risk** of all – Jawaharlal Nehru*

## A LITTLE RISQUE

**Q:** Project management is all about the management of risk. Why is it then that many projects don't even have a risk log? Surely this puts these projects at risk?

**A:** As Captain Hook said in the film 'Bad form, really bad form'. I wonder how many projects have been rejected at the pre-implementation review meeting because of the absence of risk logs. Not that many I'll wager.

What I do know is that most of us pay little more than lip service to risk management. I would guess that a high percentage of projects start off with a first-cut risk profile. It will contain the usual culprits such as risky situations around resource availability, budget overruns, lack of light-speed decision-making, customers not signing off on their latest wish list of requirements and so on and so forth. Blah-Blah-Blah!!

But actually, how many of these so-called risks can be managed by the project in isolation? What can be done at the project level? This is what we should be focusing on. The other risks just need to be escalated for resolution by the grown-ups. Get them to do something useful!

It makes sense to purely focus on any impacts to your project and that's it, job done. If you feel it helps to share the load then by all means provide a risk update at the project board as well, given it's their job to ensure a successful outcome. However, don't be disappointed if you never get round to them on the agenda as risk management always seems to be the item that never gets air-time. 'Is it finished?' always gets air time.

So once you've escalated all of the noise, then you can really focus on what's left and also look at some of the risks you may wish to take. Share

157

these ones with your sponsors and give them a best case and worse case scenario for each of them in order to get their buy in or not. Share the burden but if we all take the view that risks are only to be managed and not taken, then we are in danger of standing still and never moving forward.

When you have identified the risks that can be effectively managed, then why not work out the time and cost impacts if they materialise and include them in your schedule. Make the successor tasks clearly identifiable as not being able to start, unless the dependent risks have been mitigated and report on their progress well in advance of the dates. This should keep management interested enough as they have an overt nervousness of anything that might turn a project non-Green in colour.

Now let's go back to risk taking. What do I mean? Well all I'm really asking is that projects take a minimalist approach to what they produce both in terms of software and the accompanying documentation. Review all the deliverables that are going to be produced and sit down with the team and the support organisations that will be impacted by these decisions and then ask a couple of basic questions. Firstly and by far most importantly, ask yourself how will the customer obtain value from this deliverable or activity? Secondly, who or what is going to perish if I don't do this?

I do understand that this will not sit well with everybody. I'm sure that auditors would need a significant amount of convincing. However, if we really want to make a difference and provide outstanding service to our customers then a certain level of risk must be taken. Having a risk profile is only important if it reflects the true project impacts and what the outcomes would be if the risk materialised, and I mean the real outcomes in terms of time, cost, quality, content, exposure or customer value.

In summary then, it's not whether you have a risk log or not, but how it is being used to track risks that are taken as well as the more traditional approach to risk management. This is where the steering group needs to earn its money!

## RED RAG TO A BULL

**Q:** What is the most effective process you have used for understanding the true status of projects? I am responsible for a large portfolio of projects and am consistently embarrassed and surprised by last minute delays and excuses. We seem to have acquired a culture of weekly project reporting that goes something like: - On target, On target, On target, On target, Delayed 6 weeks. This has to stop.

**A:** This is not very good at all as not only is it causing havoc with your customers' delivery plans but is also creating a massive amount of re-planning and re-testing internally. It's also causing a major credibility issue to you personally so let's see how this can be avoided.

Well as sure as night follows day most projects will struggle; it's inevitable and must be accepted by everyone involved because no-one will admit there is a different way of doing things other than projects. There may be many reasons for this and there's no point in listing them here as you know what they are and I'll only end up going over old ground yet again.

Late surprises must not be tolerated. As soon as anything occurs on a project that may cause a potential delay or invoke a major concern, it must be flagged up to senior management. As well as raising the flag, it would be kind of nice if senior management were presented with a series of options to contain any impacts, so they can go into bat with the stakeholders armed with well thought through choices. You should not be punished for raising an issue but you should be if you try and hide it and incorrectly report the status of a project. It can cost your company huge sums of money and maybe even your job if you adopt this behaviour.

The process I am about to outline is extremely effective and can help enormously to keep projects under control. I have taken part in this personally and although I did not come up with the idea, I can vouch for its effectiveness in significantly reducing the number of projects in peril.

For argument's sake, let's call the process the weekly RAG review where RAG = Red, Amber and Green. Every project must be in one of these states as there is no room for Mr Reddish, Mr Greenish or any shade of yellow at this particular forum.

To make it easier to understand and also to nurture some lively debate I will describe each of the colours and their meaning.

**RED** – the project **will** be either late, over budget, have quality issues, scope management issues, high impact risks that cannot be mitigated or serious resource issues.

**AMBER** – the project **may** have all or some of the Red symptoms but with corrective action can be recovered. It may also be that the project manager has a concern that needs to be escalated to the review meeting and is raising this via an amber flag and will outline the concern and potential corrective actions for agreement at the meeting.

**GREEN** – everything **is** on track. Budget, timescales, quality, risks, issues, scope coverage, resources and environments will all be in place as planned. A word of advice – don't just accept this as a given. Ask a few questions when time allows as Green projects are great but in the early days of this process somewhat rarer than they will be when everyone is comfortable with the review and the way it operates.

Whether you agree with the above descriptions or not is somewhat irrelevant as it is the weekly review process that is important. You can tune the descriptions as best fits for your organisation.

Each week, approximately 48 hours before the review meeting, the latest project data is transposed on to a reporting spreadsheet that will be used at the meeting. This can be sliced and diced in any way depending on how senior management wants the meeting to run. For the purposes of this exercise, let's assume the sort sequence is project within programme of work or portfolio.

It is the responsibility of every project manager to provide the latest agreed position of their projects, usually to an individual appointed to administer the meeting. This will include some static details of the project such as name, project manager, programme manager and sponsor. The critical dynamic data such as budget (planned vs. forecast), timescales (planned vs. forecast), risks and issues (red only) and the project status is then updated each week. If your organisation has an independent function that performs health checks on projects, then their view of project status should also be incorporated and debated at the meeting if it differs from that of the project manager. Independent test and infrastructure groups should also include their view of the project status, again with any conflicting views discussed at the meeting or beforehand, with the relevant project manager.

The meeting attendees must review the latest report in advance, to get the most out of the session. This also enables the project or programme managers to clarify other groups' views where they differ from their own so as to not waste executive time at the meeting.

The meeting itself should last for 3-4 hours each week. This sounds alot but in my opinion is a very small price to pay for a customer and project-driven organisation. Attendees should be the responsible project manager and programme manager, empowered representatives of the executive business sponsor, test, infrastructure, application support and quality assurance. Project and Programme Managers need only attend for their piece of the action.

I.T. and business senior management representation is non-negotiable. Ideally this should be the individuals with overall responsibility for project delivery in both customer and supplier organisations. Experience tells me that the meeting is much more effective if these people are present. Delegation doesn't work unless it's to someone at their peer level; the meeting loses its teeth, the challenging questions diminish and word gets around very quickly that it's not important any more, whereas the opposite is true.

At the meeting, each group of projects is reviewed and it is the project managers' responsibility to present their projects, supported by their programme managers, and report any issues they need help with. For non-Green projects time-bound actions are documented and these should help move the project back to Green status. All outstanding actions are then reviewed and their latest status is updated on the review log. There must be total consensus at the end of the meeting as to the status of each project. No parking of issues is allowed.

To start this initiative, I recommend that the focus be almost exclusively on Red projects. Do not be amazed if there are many more Red projects presented at the first meeting than was first thought. There are two reasons for this. One is the newly-published description of Red, Amber and Green status. Probably for the first time ever, a consistent description is available across the organisation resulting in a level of deliberation and adjustment by the project managers. Secondly, if the delivery directors are worth their salt, they will communicate that the objective of the meeting is not to beat people up but to work as a review team to get rogue projects back on track and improve delivery performance. This is a key cultural statement from the head honchos and absolutely essential to encourage open and honest project reporting.

Once the meeting is running smoothly then gradually introduce the Amber projects and review them with the same rigour as the Red projects. They might not need the same focus but any activities undertaken to address the Amber issues will be much more pro-active and should prevent the project from ever regressing to Red status.

About once a month, it is time well spent to add an extra hour or so to the meeting and go through the Green projects and validate that they really are on track. Don't be surprised if all are not but don't assume that they are without a challenge. Remember, the I.T. Industry's track record of having truly Green projects is not good.

As time progresses, I have no doubt that the number of Red projects will reduce given the delivery focus of the review meeting. Rarely have I seen the total increase and this only happens when senior management takes one foot off the gas and attend on a less frequent basis, as opposed to anything more sinister.

This process will not necessarily stop projects getting into trouble but it will identify issues much earlier so corrective action can be taken. It will eliminate the element of surprise, reduce embarrassment and exposure and make project delivery much more visible and assured across the entire organisation.

It really works and I would recommend anyone to try it out. The only tweaks you may wish to consider is the timing of the meeting as it will obviously work better if the data under review is as near to real-time as possible. So why not pin up the latest RAG review dashboard so that every individual can see what's going on, including the customers? Perhaps use this as an opportunity to remove that condescending poster once and for all and replace it with something useful?

## WE WANT YOU AS A NEW RECRUIT – NOT CONVINCED?

**Q:** I have been searching for a new job for quite some time and am not having any luck. I have applied for over 150 jobs in the last few months. I have made absolutely sure that I meet all of the entry criteria and that this is clearly demonstrated on my CV before I apply. I have not had one single response from any of the on-line recruitment companies. Do you have any alternative suggestions? Why don't they have the courtesy to respond?

**A:** I have experienced similar frustrations I'm afraid. The recruitment companies will tell you that they are inundated with applications for every job they advertise and it would be impossible to respond to every applicant. I'm not sure what effort they put in to decide which CVs to take forward and which to reject. I'm not sure what experience many of the recruiters have in order to make an informed decision.

I have some sympathy for them but not very much. In these days of group e-mails, surely it can't be that difficult and time consuming to send out a 'Thanks but No Thanks' message to each and every applicant. That's their job isn't it? It used to be called customer service. One cannot expect a CV critique followed by a tailored personal e-mail explaining why the CV doesn't cut the mustard. That is a service that must be paid for if offered, and that's fair enough. I think we've lost the plot with the advent of on-line job sites and something is badly missing.

However, this will not change so there's absolutely no point in moaning about it. Personally, other than my first job after I left school, I have never been successful in getting an interview other than via my network of contacts. I don't think that my CV is of poor quality and I'm sure I am not alone with this experience. Some people must be getting placed as a result of on-line job advertising as companies would not get any new hires at all. One thing I do know is that the best jobs never get advertised so you need to find alternative channels. Here are some suggestions :-

- Use your network of contacts either directly or via an on-line networking or social media site. Let people know you are available and what you are looking for.

- Look back at your previous employers and try and cross sell another service. For example, if you were successful in an organisation in project delivery, make an offer to do some project assurance work so your experience can be put to good use. It may only be a few days a month but it is time well spent instead of waiting aimlessly for responses to your on-line applications. Obviously this only works for contract or part-time assignments.

- Get a quality web site built as you never get a second chance to make a first impression. Make sure there is absolute clarity about what you do, what your unique proposition is and get some references or case studies from previous successes. Don't be afraid to include a war story where things didn't quite go to plan.

- Develop some sort of newsletter and target your audience. It may be a good investment to purchase a mailing list with current e-mail addresses of decision makers.

- Target some industry publications and get a compelling article under the nose of their editors.

- Make sure that you tailor the covering letter that accompanies your CV. It must clearly explain why you would be of benefit to the company in question. Always highlight your achievements and explain how you can personally make a difference.

- Make sure your CV is succinct and maybe consider including details only for positions you've held in the last 10-15 years. I'm not keen on details of hobbies as I'm more likely to focus on them and make a Go/No Go decision for interview based on these. It's wrong I know but that's me.

- Don't give up. It is soul-destroying work I know but as you have found out, the job will not come to you, no matter how good you think you are.

# REVOLTING CUSTOMERS WITH REVENGE ON THEIR MINDS

**Q:** I am a customer of the I.T. department and I don't think I get a very good service. My company has just merged the business and I.T. into one unit as part of their annual tinkering and my new job is to kick I.T. into shape. I think we need revolution not evolution. Do you have any views on this approach?

**A:** The outcome that you need to achieve is the same as a revolution but make sure it feels like a bloodless coup to the people. Do you really need a forcible overthrow of your I.T. department in favour of a new system or would a fundamental shift in its performance be what you are looking for?

Here's what not to do!

It is common knowledge that most change or transformation programmes fail to deliver everything that they set out to achieve. In many cases I've seen them make matters worse.

For some unknown reason it seems to be common practice to employ a large army of consultants. They come in, spend huge amounts of money, play the change card to gain access to all areas as if it's a high security badge and then leave the company not a whole lot better off than it was. Most people end up with their mouths wide open wondering 'What happened there?' So please avoid doing that. It really isn't necessary.

Revolutions are never successful if you patronise the I.T. people. Comments like 'Things are going to be done a lot differently round here from now on' tend to be met with blank looks and mutterings of 'Here we go again'. Also best to avoid posters and newsletters telling them how great it's going to be. That's not good; not good at all.

Other things that will not work include: -

- Removing contingency from plans – especially for revenge purposes.
- Reducing estimates to make schedules look easier on the eye.
- Doing the estimating yourself.
- Not allowing quality activities into the schedule.
- Brown bag lunches.

- Compulsory communication away days.
- Shouting.

I'm not saying you shouldn't try any of these things but they won't deliver the revolution you are seeking.

So what will? If you only do one thing and one thing only, it must be to ensure that every activity performed in your organisation by I.T. adds value to what gets delivered to your stakeholders. Don't waste your time doing anything that doesn't. Stop it and do something that does. Yes I know I'm repeating myself but if the reader only gets one or two things from this book then I'd like this to be one of them.

Areas where I have seen order of magnitude improvements include: -

- Introduction of agile and lean methods.
- Insisting on removal of defects as early as possible.
- Reduction in non-essential documentation.
- Lighter and much more fit-for-purpose processes.
- Automation of as much testing as possible.
- Re-use of existing assets – although this should have gone better than it did in the history of I.T!
- Empower the teams to plan and track their own work – trust them!
- Get project managers to manage and not interfere too much with non-management activities.
- Appoint an inspiring and respected leader.
- Focus on projects that only add value to the business and ban pet projects. It may well be that a particular business function gets no new projects for a year. A bitter pill to swallow maybe but so what? If money is better targeted elsewhere then so be it.
- Ask your team what needs improving. Trust me, they will know. And then, get them to do the work. It's amazing what results you achieve when people feel valued, engaged and trusted.

It's a wild stab in the dark but I'm guessing that this is not the answer you were either expecting or looking for but hey - Sssshhhh…. I.T. happens!

**S**

*'I don't know the key to **Success**, but the key to failure is trying to please everybody' – Bill Cosby*

**SHORT SHARP SHOCK TREATMENT**

This chapter is all about quick-fire Q&A's; an almighty confusion of S.

**Q:** While I was waiting to be seen by my dentist I read an article in a magazine about software being a dangerous artefact. Is this true?

**A:** Good quality software is not dangerous at all as it always does what it says on the tin. Poor quality software on the other hand can be a real risk to people's livelihoods and very much the danger that the magazine article is alluding to. Just think about it for a second. Software is pervasive in aircraft, in automobiles, in hospitals, in banks, in heating systems, in power plants and in weaponry. In fact almost everything today has an element of software embedded within it. There have been many disasters attributable to software defects that are readily accessible on the Internet should you wish to find out more details. Proceed with due care and attention and do not compromise on quality. This will keep the streets safe and make it more difficult for people to act maliciously.

**Q:** What constitutes a successful software project?

**A:** First and foremost, one that needs to be done; one that adds real value to the customer's business. Other important factors include how you did against cost, time and quality targets but this is the case with every project. The business features that are delivered need not be precisely what was requested as long as the key ingredients are there, so only build what the customers' need, which is quite often vastly different to what they thought they wanted originally. Obviously you will need to demonstrate any newly acquired influencing and negotiating skills here.

Another important factor is learning. What valuable information do we now have as an organisation that is purely attributable to this project? If there are any nuggets that would benefit others then share these insights across the organisation.

Finally, the customers must be delighted with the solution of course, which probably means that it works without vast amounts of support to prop things up, performs satisfactorily and adds real value to their day-to-day business.

**Q:** Are I.T. Strategy and Architecture groups a good thing?

**A:** It depends. I'm not sure what makes someone a good strategist or architect. I guess if your organisation has a legacy from hell inasmuch as every project needs to cater for hundreds of systems that may be impacted by a change, or if the annual portfolio of projects continues to eat vast amounts of money without any real improvements or cost reductions, then the answer is no, it's pointless having them. If there is a clear technical roadmap to Utopia and it will be followed and adhered to, then that's good isn't it?

**Q:** Why are there so many reported security issues with data and software? How can these be avoided?

**A:** Given the sophistication of today's hackers and pirates, I don't think it is possible to completely wipe it out. Certainly a good start would be to not trust people with information that gets left behind on public transport, airport lounges or hotel lobbies. I have to ask the question 'Why on earth was this confidential information allowed out to play in the first place?'

As software systems have become more complex and massively scalable, it is simply not possible to test every branch in every program to ensure it is secure and performing as required. This would take many lifetimes. However, it is much more difficult to cause damage to a system that has been designed with quality and security in mind.

All that you can do is have a zero tolerance of defects, design your system so that it is as secure as it can possibly be and put yourself in the position of somebody who wants to create havoc when you are testing it.

**Q:** I run a commercial software company that provides products and services to the stock markets around the world. How can I ensure my survival in a recession?

**A:** Firstly, ensure that you maintain a compelling offer that proves irresistible to your customer base whatever the market conditions.

Secondly, ensure you have a competitive edge. Your software products must perform in line with what it says on the box in terms of content, quality, security and performance.

Thirdly, always hit your dates, whatever type of release you are pushing to the market but never compromise on quality.

Finally, I would be surprised if you can ethically charge your customers for fixing any defects in your products. So why not be pro-active and update your marketing material and offer to fix any defects that are attributable to your software, wait for it, free of charge. This is not that much of a risk if you focus on delivering quality software. It only becomes a matter of survival if you have more people working on fixing defects than building new functionality or opening up new markets.

**Q:** I have been invited to present at a seminar in a couple of months. It's not something I've ever done before and was wondering if you have any advice?

**A:** I'm not sure that I'm the right person to answer the question as I've only done this on a couple of occasions. I'd like to say it was a walk in the park but that would not be telling the whole truth and nothing but the truth. I learned that I must never ever consider public speaking as a career. I am rubbish at it! However I did pick up a few pointers along the way that I will share with you now: -

> ➤ Don't have too many slides – a rough guide is 1 slide per 2 minutes of presentation so if you have a 45 minute slot, I would have a maximum of 15-18 slides leaving time at the end for questions.
> ➤ Don't have too much noise on the slide. Music and flashy slides are all very well and really great when they come off. They often don't, so why risk embarrassment as people will have come to

listen to what you have to say rather than be dazzled by your artistic prowess.

➢ Keep the wording on the slide to a minimum. Don't put up slides where there is literally no space for any more words. Engage with your audience, maintain eye contact with them - not the slide and have a few stories to tell that will break the session up from being purely a slide show presentation.

➢ Rehearse your presentation and know your subject matter deeply. Be prepared for some detailed questions and the inevitable curved ball.

➢ Start on time and finish on time. You can always leave contact details with your audience or even arrange to meet them afterwards at another venue within the seminar location for further discussions or even socially!

➢ Know your audience. Ask them what roles they perform by a show of hands and if the attendees are from many countries, avoid colloquialisms. You will lose them totally as I found out the hard way.

➢ Finally, relax and try and enjoy it. If you relay your passion for the subject then your audience will respond with very positive feedback. Good Luck.

**Q:** We have many standards within our organisation. That's good isn't it?

**A:** As long as they are known, available and evolving to meet current needs then yes it is. If they are purely to satisfy the whim of an auditor or an extreme process fundamentalist then it's no good at all. In fact I would say they are dangerous, job creating and innovation-stifling if this were the case. To be effective the standard needs to be fairly generic inasmuch as it encourages local modification to meet the needs of the project or way of working. That's it really. Quite straightforward you'd think?

**Q:** Why do our suppliers continue to deliver late and with poor quality? I thought the opposite would be true?

**A:** Why on earth would you think the opposite is true? Have the suppliers' deliverables been through a sheep dip that will automatically cleanse them of defects and conform to exactly what was specified? Are their developers technically superior to yours? Did the due diligence and selection processes discover anything useful at all?

170

I do apologise as I'm not having a pop at you. This, sadly, happens all too frequently in my experience, so what are the causes and how do you stop it?

1. Use an industry strength supplier selection process and ensure your requests for information contain questions around quality as well as delivery precision. Ask them for their defect density data as this invariably attracts some noise and concern; however the response is usually quite amusing and will give an early indication of their maturity.

2. Visit potential suppliers' reference sites. Focus on the acceptance effort required and how much time they have to spend fixing defects and re-testing software that has already been paid for? Ask very awkward and challenging questions e.g. How long does it take you to implement a delivery and what are the main issues?

3. Ensure the contract is outcome based in your favour. Incorporate penalties for poor quality and late delivery as well as a few rewards for great quality and early delivery.

4. Ask them what they are doing in the improvement space, in terms of productivity and quality. How are their estimating. planning and tracking activities evolving? How do they learn as an organisation?

5. Include something in the contract around rotation of staff. Your investment is also in their people and you may have spent a considerable amount of time, effort and money to familiarise them with your business. The last thing you need is for the supplier to remove them from your account once they have acquired expert knowledge.

6. If the supplier has a high maturity rating, such as CMMI Level 5, ask them how this equates to the team working on your account. It may have been achieved in a different part of the same organisation. This may not be a major issue but you need to know what you are getting.

7. Remember always that they are suppliers and not partners.

8. Ensure your own organisation improves its processes around software acquisition and acceptance throughout the development lifecycle. Ensure you track the suppliers' activities as you would do your own to avoid any nasty surprises. Include them in your weekly projects review.

9. Never forget that you have not outsourced any risks as far as your customers are concerned. They will not care who performs the activities as long as they get a great service, so the risk is still with you.

10. Finally, continue to browse the market place and exploit new entrants who may be able to offer something different. This will avoid complacency in your existing supplier base, as you will no doubt mention you are doing this when you next speak to them.

# T

*'Any sufficiently advanced **Technology** is indistinguishable from magic'* – *Arthur C. Clarke*

## TIME FOR A REFRESHING CHANGE

Given that this is a book about information technology and its people, it would be remiss of me to treat the 'T for Technology' section in the same way as all the others and so I haven't.

I often wonder what it would be like if we were governed by the technocrats of the world. For those who aren't aware, a technocracy is a form of government where decisions and policy-making are attributed to technical experts in their respective fields. This does not assume any political ability or communication skills whatsoever.

Government bodies would be populated entirely by solution providers and problem solvers. How could this fail? So, just imagine 650 technical people in the same room debating the issues of the day, waving papers and shouting 'Order Order'. Prime Minister's Questions would be very entertaining.

Before we start I have a word of warning. The threat of the technocracy being infiltrated by their customers is high. If this insurgency were to materialise, there would be an immediate reduction in the number of members to probably half the existing amount, as apparently I.T. always doubles its estimates. The other noticeable sign would be the removal of all contingency plans for any event whatsoever. This would be viewed as the technocrats over-engineering again, so we need to be on our guard.

Before forming a government though, there would need to be an election of some description. As a pre-requisite, a robust and realistic manifesto would need to be produced in order to win over a suspicious public. These could be its main constituents:-

**IMMEDIATE INTRODUCTION OF IDENTITY CARDS**

These would be introduced with immediate effect, or certainly within 20% of immediate effect, and without any consultation with anyone. It would be a criminal offence to be caught without an identity card, punishable by 30 minutes in a broken lift with an engineer who only knows machine code. Deterrent enough methinks!

The following data would be held on an embedded chip on the card: -

- Actual Name or Ridiculous Nickname.
- TCP/IP Home Address.
- Laptop Serial Number in Modulus 11.
- Age in hexadecimal.
- Favourite COBOL verb.
- Date of last haircut.
- Total Number of wings picked off insects during adolescence.
- Date that you last cancelled a training course.
- Number of testers verbally abused by you in a calendar year.
- Number of defects removed from someone else's code this month.
- Name of the last project manager that you ignored.
- Time of last grunt when anybody spoke to you.
- Weight of last technical document written.
- Name of last user that you confused the hell out of.
- Date when last properly cooked meal eaten.
- Favourite programming manual (must be scrawled on).
- Date that you last photocopied a manual in less than 24 hours.
- Best Star Trek character, ever.
- Last time someone annoyed you.
- Last time you produced a banded estimate where the band was > 1.
- Y/N indicator that states whether you believe the music died in 1979.

- Y/N indicator which states whether you believe the Y/N indicator has other values other than Yes or No (S for sometimes perhaps).

## NEW MINISTRY OF EXPENSES CREATED IN FIRST PARLIAMENT

Every household must retain at least three different estimates for every job to be carried out by an accredited external contractor. These must be kept for a minimum of 7 years in an off-site fireproof safe from where it must be virtually impossible to retrieve them. In addition, all supermarket receipts must be retained in triplicate, for up to 2 years, accompanied by a traceability matrix so that any previous expense claims can be cross-referenced.

Members' expenses will only be authorised if they contain mileage, travel, subsistence, accommodation or pizza.

Any member who has to stay away in an hotel on business must retain evidence of the stay by handing over the following acquisitions to support their claim. Please remember this is policy and non-negotiable: -

- A single chocolate (unwrapped) from the hotel bed pillow.
- A shower cap (unused and in its original plastic bag).
- A needlework set (boxed – but some of it may have been used).
- Shampoo (preferably blue in colour in a small see-through plastic bottle).
- Orange Shower Gel (product packaged as per Shampoo).
- Soap (unused, boxed and at least 2 years out of date).
- Unopened packets of coffee, tea, hot chocolate, sugar and shortbread biscuits.
- Out of date but complimentary magazines and newspapers.
- Dressing gown (must contain original security tag).

## REVOLUTIONARY TAX CHANGES

A new negative tax, called an engineering discount, will be introduced with immediate effect and will apply to all take away food purchased between the hours of 11pm and 7am, 7 days a week, 365 days of the year. Leap years are not recognised in this particular technocracy.

This means that all food will be subject to an anti-tax discount of up to 10%, payable in ridiculously designed vouchers resembling raffle tickets. These can only be redeemed for the purchase of technical manuals, science fiction DVDs, computer games and pizza. Any restaurant or food establishment that refuses to sell pizza on a takeaway basis will be subject to Pizza Avoidance Tax (PAT) as well as a naming and shaming in the House.

Other tax changes include: -

- Abolition of corporation tax for any technicians working through a limited company, where they are the only director.
- Tax discounts based on the number of defect-free programs implemented, as measured by a nominated preferred customer.
- Free rentals of Star Trek, Star Wars and Doctor Who DVDs for life.
- 20% tax increase for managers and testers, maybe more for testers, not sure yet!
- 50% tax on all earnings for anyone admitting to being a consultant.
- On the spot fines for anyone using the words guru, traction, away day, quick win, in terms of, challenge or devil's advocate. Anyone running anything up any flagpole whatsoever will be subject to a verbal warning. If any interest is shown by anybody as to what salutes it, this will be dealt with more severely. Details to follow.

**EDUCATION AND TRAINING**

This will be the significant sea change. Anyone with a degree in Computer Science will be treated with the utmost respect and they will take a seat for life in the technocracy upper chamber. Lack of any communication skills will not be allowed to inhibit this progression. Members who attain 'upper chamber status' will never ever be consulted on any subject whatsoever.

Any project or programme management accreditations or certificates that have previously been awarded for less than 1 or 2 weeks effort by a member will become invalid. Recruitment companies will be banned from requesting evidence of these on job advertisements and instead, it will become mandatory to read CVs and talk to prospective job applicants about their experience prior to rejection. Interviews will be carried out on behalf of the agencies, at their expense, by experienced practitioners in order to preclude wasting anybody's time and money.

All software degrees and courses must incorporate a module about software quality and how individual developers can plan, track and remove defects from their work at the same time as learning contemporary languages and techniques. In this way standards will be raised, quality will improve and customers will get a much better bang for their buck. This is a rare serious policy statement.

## MINISTRY OF DEFENCE

All conflicts will be halted immediately and any residual 'misunderstandings' will be resolved by nominated protagonists, preferably one from each side, in a best of 3 World of War game on a mutually agreed social media site. This will lead to world peace, harmony and massive savings in every country's defence budget. These savings can then be used to fund I.T. projects where no technician will ever be unemployed, irrespective of their ability.

However, as this technical defence strategy will take some time to bed in and gain worldwide acceptance, a tactical stopgap is required in order to ameliorate any terrorist threat. Solution providers and technical experts will be trained in negotiating skills and then released into the wild to talk to terrorist leaders. That should stop them.

## MORE NEW MINISTRIES WILL SPRING UP IN LATER SESSIONS

The technocracy think-tank will be granted three years to brainstorm the need for new functions but they must include: -

**MINISTRY OF HYGIENE** – includes incentives for daily baths or showers being taken by all members. Haircuts will be mandatory once both eyes are totally covered. Any expense claims for soap and deodorant will be looked on favourably.

**MINISTRY OF CULTURE** – this bureaucratic mumbo-jumbo of a department will be created to ensure that any cultural change initiative has something in it for the technicians. Tools of the trade, a desk and nearness to a window will be high on any early agendas.

**MINISTRY OF MEASUREMENT** – members of this ministry will be recognisable by their uniforms. Tweed jackets with a leather elbow patch on the left sleeve will be the order of the day. Badges that clearly state 'If you can't measure it then you can't manage it' must be worn at all times. Archives will be created with details of every project in the world, how many function points it created, why it was late with free-form narrative in the section of the report marked 'Why doesn't anybody listen to us?'

**MINISTRY OF BIG BUDGETS** – it is unclear at this stage whether this will be aligned with anything at all and until the situation becomes clearer, the technocracy will continue to award huge I.T. contracts to the same companies who have previously failed spectacularly to deliver anything useful.

**SOCIAL SECRETARY OF STATE** – this is not to be confused with the state of the social secretary; a common misunderstanding. This is a brand new post with far reaching powers to arrange techno-socials. We are not sure what a techno-social is but we hope it will be a vast improvement on the previous incarnation where huge sums of money were wasted on discos and buffets, where very few people showed up and those that did sat at their tables all night staring into space. We have had a handful of suggestions as to what themes may attract attendance from technical members and these are they: -

1. A 3-hour presentation, with nibbles, on the strategic use of .NET.
2. Paint-balling where the winning team receive a complete set of Java manuals.
3. Simulation of a project where the testers don't set the status to RED before any work has been perfomed.
4. Throwing tomatoes at the management team while they are securely locked in stocks in the town square.
5. Star Trek themed evening.

Well that's it folks and I think you will agree that it is a recipe for strong government where few decisions are made, funds are allocated based on no consultation whatsoever and absolutely nothing runs on time.

178

An era of change where it is absolutely acceptable to spend the entire year writing the perfect computer program and where everything is measured to the nth degree and those nasty agile zealots and lean thinkers stay indoors.

# U

*'The only thing that makes life possible is permanent, intolerable* **Uncertainty**, *not knowing what comes next – Ursula K. LeGuin*

## UNDER THE COSH

**Q:** Do you have advice in how to survive an economic downturn? I own a small software development company and am obviously concerned about sustaining my business in these uncertain times.

**A:** With the risk of repeating myself, these are challenging times and I hope that any company that strives to deliver outstanding work for their customers manages to survive. I do hope you have managed to build a war chest when conditions weren't so tough.

I can only realistically address this from a software perspective, given that I have no clue about economics or running a business. Some people who know me well may even challenge my grasp of the software world. However, that won't stop me making some suggestions.

Firstly I would ensure that I strove relentlessly to keep everybody in the company performing chargeable work. No matter how much you may wish it otherwise, there are likely to be some casualties in a downturn and sadly these may well be overheads that you can no longer afford. You may even be able to offer a small reduction in costs to your customers as they will be feeling the pinch as well.

Next I would take a look at quality. If you are spending a lot of time on re-work that the customer will not pay for, then this will kill you, and so it would be good to address any problems here. Start collecting some data in this area and review the outcome as this often comes as a nasty surprise.

Of equal importance is ensuring that your schedules are under control. Are you meeting your dates? Is your customer happy with your delivery performance? If not get to the bottom of the problem and address it quickly. The last thing you need is dissatisfied customers.

Cashflow is even more critical in tough times. Customers who may previously have been happy to pay their invoices on time or even earlier, may not be so forthcoming in a downturn and may even ask for longer to pay. This will seriously challenge the small company. To counter this, try and look at other ways of raising funds with your existing customers. Maybe cross selling a service or taking on some support or maintenance work, could help to ease things a little.

You should also look to get personally involved in the sales and marketing activities. Review your offerings and what sales channels you are using. Are you getting the most out of your website? Is it clear exactly what you are selling and do you have a compelling message for prospective customers? Have you asked your existing customers for references that you can use as case studies? How about developing a regular newsletter or blog showing what you are up to - with some success stories?

Just a few ideas and at the risk of sounding patronising, now may be a good time to heed the words of Benjamin Franklin who said 'In this world nothing can be said to be certain, except death and taxes'. I'd also add that software development will always be a challenging service to sell.

## UP IN THE CLOUDS

**Q:** Are you upbeat about the future of the I.T. industry?

**A:** Very much so. When I look back to when I started work in the London branch of a U.S bank in the early seventies, not many people had even heard of computers in my neck of the woods.

I remember fondly the first computer that I was trained to operate. It was enormous. It's a bit like your first love. You are not too sure what to do with it but it definitely looks and feels good. A completely partitioned room had to be built with air-conditioning units that used to freeze up in hot weather. Fortunately it was London so this was a rare occurrence. It possessed a massive 20K of main memory with printing facilitated by a paper tape loop that we punched holes in according to some DIY instructions provided by the programmers. Programs were compiled from punched cards and then output to yet more paper tape. These were pink in colour, with grey remaining the domain of the printer loops.

In hindsight this was prehistoric, but to me it felt like I was on the bleeding edge of technology. The thing I liked most about my computer was that it was blue, clean and usually quite reliable as long as I cleaned the disk heads regularly with some lethal alcoholic liquid and vacuumed the printer a few times a day. This was my baby and I did not mind one bit.

Nearly 40 years on from this, the world of technology is unrecognisable. The progress has been staggering and I see no reason why this trend will not continue. The hardware industry, on an almost annual basis, continues to deliver an order of magnitude improvement in both price and performance. The software industry has not kept pace with this but I do believe things are improving and will continue to do so. We've spoken enough about the quality problem and I think there is an awareness out there that certainly wasn't there even a decade ago.

The software industry is relatively new. As time has progressed, the world has become ever more reliant on software. It is difficult to think of many artefacts that we come into contact with on a daily basis that don't have some level of embedded software to make them work.

The downside is that software can be viewed as a dangerous artefact in itself, if it is not developed properly. It is much easier to act maliciously if you are trying to hack into a system that is riddled with defects or lacks the relevant security controls. This does not mean that it needs to take a long time to build and require huge amounts of documentation and bureaucracy. It is simply something that always works as it has been built with fit for purpose processes.

I am really encouraged by the take-up of agile methods. I have never personally managed a project using any of these methods but I find the focus on delivery and what the customer values as very compelling and upbeat. It makes complete sense. Waterfall methods still have their place but are really only applicable when it is fairly obvious that all the requirements are known in advance and there can be little opportunity for change.

There is a view that quality assurance activities or project planning are inappropriate in the agile world but I don't believe this for one second. I'm sure our customers may well be delighted that projects are being delivered quicker and changes, even late changes to requirements, are embraced but I will guarantee that this euphoria would be short-lived if the system availability was below standard due to software defects. Time-boxing activity requires discipline and rigour although many believe otherwise, so why not time-box your quality activities? You can still perform them early thus enhancing the Agile image but don't ditch them as you will come unstuck as you approach implementation.

I think history will look on the last part of the 20th century as the building blocks for another industrial revolution. The advent of the Internet and social media, not all of it good, has revolutionised people's daily routine. Technical advances have been staggering. My son has a gadget that has a massive amount of storage, can play music, games and videos at will and will happily fit in the top pocket of his shirt. What next – Clouds perhaps?

It is the 'what next' that makes me feel upbeat about I.T. I'm sure that in ten years time it will be even more unrecognisable. This coupled with the enthusiasm and intelligence of everybody who works in it, makes it such a rewarding place to work.

What would I like to see? How about a product that can scan A4 requirements, design and generate source code and produce a list of all requirements which are ambiguous, un-testable, un-implementable and clearly ridiculous for the job in hand. It must then trace the requirements, tri-dimensionally if necessary, through the design and code, then report on the success of the trace. It must be able to interrogate the design to ensure conformance to standards and architecture and then produce a menu of re-use opportunities. It will then re-factor the code, automatically removing defects and identify code that will never be executed or is inefficiently written. It will add comments in five different languages and hide them behind the successor to the animated paper clip. Finally it will output a smug ring-tone and a smiley face that clearly demonstrates how clever it is and how stupid we humans are. This is just the first step. Revolution will occur when the product can converse with a customer, elicit their requirements and then design and code a solution for their review within 24 hours.

What will the I.T. people do? We will write books, attend reunion events and ride on unicorns instead!

## UNDER THE SPOTLIGHT

**Q:** What is your most unforgettable work experience and why?

**A:** Given that as I am writing this, I am approaching my 60th birthday, I had better make it a fairly recent experience to preclude the memory playing any tricks. On the other hand, I will not make it too recent as the ravages of short-term memory loss (STML) may kick in. In order to spend a wee while longer avoiding the question, I will conclude this answer with a career changing experience I had in Amsterdam in 1996. Hopefully this teasing promise of revelations to come will encourage you to read on. So, enough padding; let's go.

A couple of years ago I was invited to head up a team to deliver the I.T. components (both hardware and software) in support of a major financial services provider's strategy, to simplify its technology landscape and reduce its costs. This involved significant engagement with a third party who was contractually obliged to take on the data according to an agreed migration schedule and then take day-to-day operational responsibility for administration of the migrated products.

When the contract was initially signed I had no management team in place, so one of the first jobs was to trawl through CVs, (and yes I did read them), and arrange interviews via the respective recruitment agencies. I knew what I wanted in terms of the management style for each of the 5 vacancies but as there was no time to get everybody together in an assessment centre, I had absolutely no idea as to how they would gel as a team.

After a month or so I had most of the team in place and things started to take shape. As with any large organisation there was a certain amount of nervousness as we were releasing customer data to a third party and you wouldn't believe how many people crawled out of the woodwork calling 'Foul' in the early days. The Borrowers made a late appearance from behind the skirting boards although their concern was understandable as at the time there was a spate of confidential information being left on buses, trains and in hotel lobbies. There were also data security and business protection issues to consider. So the project was not without its distractions irrespective of the technical complexity being undertaken.

This is just one example of the curved balls being thrown and it was no mean feat to reach first base. As time progressed I was completely amazed as to how much fun, respect, trust and sheer hard work could take place on a critical project. The results were astonishing. We had no real process to follow and were very much flying by the seat of our pants but as a team we acted as a unit, with total support for each other.

It taught me a very strong lesson that irrespective of how much individual talent one may possess, it is insignificant when a high performing team starts to fire on all six cylinders. There were many occasions when I looked in amazement and scratched my head as problem after problem was solved collectively by a team of people who months ago didn't know the others existed.

Needless to say the project was a great success not just from the I.T. side but also more importantly for our customers and project managers in the business organisation. A real team effort that ended up with the overall programme receiving an award from the parent company based on its contribution to group strategy.

One very useful by-product was, given the locations involved, there was a lot of working away from home, so we had time to get to know each other socially which helped us to bond even further as a team. The team have now gone their separate ways but we make every effort to keep in touch and I would grab any opportunity to reform the team and undertake another massive challenge with them.

However it remains unclear to me as to what influence I had on the outcome. I tend to take the approach that you need to build a fantastic team of talented people around you, empower them and don't meddle too much in what they are up to. One proviso though was that I was always there for them if they wanted to escalate anything or use me as a sounding board for their new ideas. Otherwise it was their show which allowed me to get involved in other improvement initiatives that the company were undertaking. It was the most productive and rewarding of experiences, and one that is difficult to match.

Now back to 1996 and Amsterdam. I apologise for keeping you waiting and I'm sure you will feel tremendously let down when I explain why it was so unforgettable. I'm afraid it was work-related.

I attended a conference that was being held for the first time in Europe. There were two imminent international events that needed attendance by my programme at the time. My boss and I tossed a coin to decide who went to Amsterdam and who went to California, as we agreed to share our tremendous burdens on expenses. I thought I'd drawn the short straw with Amsterdam when the coin came down 'tails' but it turned out to be an inspired call of 'heads' from yours truly.

The theme of the conference was Software Process Improvement. It doesn't sound like the greatest show in town, does it? The conference was designed to last 4 days with 2 days of half-day tutorials followed by 2 days of multi-tracked conference presentations from experts and industry practitioners alike.

It entirely changed my approach to my job and crystallised all of the things where I couldn't explain why they weren't working for me. I learned about planning and tracking; about defect removal; about independent quality assurance; the necessity to manage and trace requirements; the need to manage baselines of code, documentation and requirements so everyone is working on the right thing at the right time; the absolutely critical activity of managing suppliers and not expecting them to deliver a perfect solution without significant oversight from the Mother Ship. I also learned a lot about measurement and making sure you have a good estimating process and the ability to size the software you are building before you start building it.

Since then I've also made many mistakes and have fallen into the process trap where I've allowed the development process to take priority over the project delivery schedule. I did this once and it will never happen again. It was embarrassing.

What else have I learned since that Eureka moment?

- A model is a model – a framework for improvement – it needs to be used properly but at the end of the day it's just a model.
- Processes can be documented on one page of A4 paper. It is not necessary to judge the quality of a process purely based on how much it weighs.
- Delivery of value to the customer is more important than anything else.
- Project tracking is very powerful and equally as important as defect removal.
- Working in an agile way does not mean anarchy.

187

I won't forget that first conference. I've been to many of the same since but none of them have come close to having the profound impact on me that the very first one did. Sadly a number of snake oil salesmen have infiltrated this space over the last 10-15 years and it's sort of ruined it for me, so I no longer attend conferences or engage in software process improvement.

# TALES OF THE UNEXPECTED

**Q:** Do you have any unusual stories you can share with us? It would be preferable if they could be repeated in front of children and without threat of litigation.

**A:** I will have you know that all my stories can be told to my three grandchildren apart from the one about the apple pie, which is not mentioned here, so relax.

We have reached the stage of the book when I can see the finishing line so I'm really pleased to deal with a question that has absolutely no connection to I.T. whatsoever other than the origin of the stories have been funded by my 'Let's See The World On Expenses' campaigns.

I'm not sure everybody will find these observations unusual. I certainly did at the time and even with the benefit of hindsight I still find them a little strange. Some observations remain unanswered in terms of 'Why would you?'

Let's start with one of many visits to the French capital. Dirty work I know...

**Business class flight from Paris (CDG) to London (LHR) 1987** – as airports go I consider Charles De Gaulle to be pretty soulless. When I checked in for one of my many flights home, I was asked whether I required a smoking or non-smoking seat. As I didn't stop smoking until 14$^{th}$ April 1994, not that I'm counting, I asked for a smoking seat although as it's only a short hop across the English Channel, it would have been no big deal if there weren't any left. In fact the flight was so short in length that you collected your champagne and cardboard croissant from the stewardess at the top of the steps as you boarded.

I felt very sorry for the non-smokers, as there were 4 rows of seats in the business class section. Rows 1 & 3 were smoking seats with the other two being non-smoking. So where does the non-smoking bit come into it. Very strange, in fact one might call it business as unusual (BAU).

Next I must mention the Boys go to Brazil tour from the Eighties.

**Business class flight from London (LHR) to Sao Paulo (somewhere in Brazil) 1988 followed by a 3-week Treasury strategy study** – this still ranks as my one and only trip to Latin America. You could say I had my eyes opened. So what was unusual? A number of things spring to mind: -

- On arrival in Brazil I collected my luggage and, along with my colleague and partner in beer, made my way to the exit where a ride into town awaited. However prior to going through the exit gate everybody had to press a button that resulted in either a Green Light or a Red Light with flashing sirens and lashings of arm waving. If the light flashed Green, an ominous looking policeman rushed you through with the help of a semi-automatic pistol waving in the air. If, however, the light turned Red, I noticed some very odd behaviour.

  Whilst still in line, the entire contents of one's luggage were strewn all over the floor and inspected by armed policemen followed by a request to repack, pronto, if there was nothing suspicious in the contents. This could be somewhat embarrassing for people depending on what fell out of the suitcase. I prefer sniffer dogs if it was drugs they were searching for! I found this whole process unusual.

- Another unusual experience centred on the consumption of the national dish – Feijoada. Originally imported from Portugal, it is made from meat (not sure what meat) and black turtle beans. It tasted good but as I ate it my stomach, quite disconcertingly, started to inch its way towards the table in a most unusual way. I then spent the rest of the afternoon lying down in my hotel room as the turtle beans exploded and popped in my stomach. The only thing I could think of to counteract this strange sensation was cold, amber, fizzy and contained 5% alcohol. It was indeed a miracle cure!

- As we were in the country for 3 weeks, this meant that we had two full weekends to do a bit of sightseeing. Although it was early spring when we were there, the temperature often rose nicely during the day but certainly not when we were there. Aforementioned Beer Buddy is a weather jinx. On our first free weekend we went to a picture postcard resort on the Sao Paulo coast. We were driven down there from the city centre by what I can only describe as a complete and utter maniac. It did not occur

190

to him that tyres make a squealing noise when they don't have traction. It was of no surprise to me when I was informed that a high percentage of road traffic accidents occur in Brazil or that they produce unbelievably good racing drivers! It goes some way to explaining why there was such a large percentage of Paulistas limping around the city in plaster.

As usual I digress. The heavens opened spectacularly from the moment we arrived at the resort and did not stop until we left the hotel on the Sunday evening to head back to the city. The following weekend we went to Rio. The temperature was in the low eighties but it was shady on the side of the street we were walking on and not only that, when we crossed over to the sunny side, weather jinx took his shirt off and the sun went in. I kid you not! This, apparently, was construed by the locals as 'unusual'.

I could carry on but this would then make this a travel guide. Perhaps this could be the subject of another book called 'My Travels on Expenses'.

Other highlights would include: -

- Colleagues being hypnotised in a Paris hotel bar which angered one of our colleagues so much he smashed a glass table (I was not present m'lord).
- Explaining to a Californian waiter that red wine and ice aren't a marriage made in heaven.
- A Tapas bar lunch in Madrid between 4-6pm – hic!
- Nearly losing my fingers while sailing on the Baltic Sea.
- A search for a bottle of beer in Copenhagen that didn't cost the equivalent of my monthly mortgage repayments.
- Sailing on Lake Geneva instead of attending the conference sessions.
- Getting lost in Miami – a dangerous pursuit.
- Sightseeing in Monte Carlo from the inside of a taxi and never being able to get out of it to take a closer look.
- Discovering that bars in Brussels do not close at 11pm in 1977 – wow moment!

A very enjoyable time was had by all.

# V

*'Computer **Viruses** are an urban myth' – Peter Norton*

## VALUABLES

**Q:** From a work perspective what values do you cherish the most?

**A:** I am assuming that what you mean is 'how work gets done' as opposed to 'what work gets done'. It is imperative that everyone understands this distinction. There is little point in focusing exclusively on the 'what and when' as people won't feel motivated or valued and this is not where you want to be at all.

People like to feel trusted and listened to. They need a value system in which to operate effectively and it is management's responsibility to provide this framework. Some places even split their appraisal rewards equally between delivering against objectives and how one went about it (i.e. measured against the company's values). These are forward thinking organisations that actually are investing in their people and they will reap great benefits. The place will have a buzz and an environment for doing great work will be created once people really believe that management is serious. It is not about being kind or nice to people; it's all about being fair, honest and open with them.

I'm not sure whether the following are good values but they have evolved over my career and now form the ethics that underpin the way I work. I certainly didn't start out with these in mind and have made many mistakes along the way. I believe they have been eradicated purely based on working in a different way; the way that works best for me and my teams.

**Customers** – every task that is carried out in any organisation must have a customer and a supplier otherwise we would all be working for our own benefit. If there is any activity at all in your organisation that is not adding value to your customer, then stop doing it immediately. This applies to development work, process, documentation, communication or anything. It

192

is difficult enough doing what the customers need without wasting time on things that are of no use to them. This is about the sixth time I've mentioned this but it is so important.

**Feedback** – this is critical. Feedback is an awful word but I can't think of a better one that explains what I mean. We need to be letting our people know what we think about what they do, what they write and how they behave. Thank you costs nothing but often means everything. The timing of it is critical as well. Don't wait until a regular review of performance to let someone know when they have done well or where improvement is necessary. Do it at the time. Treat people with a refreshing attitude of openness and honesty, irrespective of whether it is good or bad news, and they will respond. They may not enjoy all of it, but they will think about it and generally act upon it.

**Communication** – there is very little in any organisation that is actually top secret irrespective of what management will have you believe. Tell your people what's going on and do it face to face. Newsletters have a place but can often be found in the recently deleted items folders of your team's inboxes. Create an opportunity for questions to be asked and answered. If you don't know the answer or it is one of those rare occasions that you can't give the answer just yet then say so, but let your people know when you will be in a position to. It's an I.T. organisation and not the secret service.

**Fun** – well definitely not the secret service then! We spend a massive percentage of our lives in the workplace. You will think I'm losing it but I strongly believe it is management's responsibility to create an environment where people can have fun and do great work at the same time. This does not mean we have to dress up as clowns. Fun is when you have been given a challenging assignment and been trusted to get on with it. When people feel trusted and empowered they do their best work.

**Stand up and be counted** – if something isn't working then say so. If your project has hit a brick wall and may be delayed then say so. If people are not delivering on the commitments that they have previously agreed to and often proposed themselves, then say so. My management mantra dictates that nobody will be thought less of if they say what they think but they will be if they don't, as soon as the issues arise.

**Play to your strengths** – always accept roles that are challenging but exploit your strengths. If you are not comfortable with the inter-personal

193

side of things, then work as hard as you can to overcome this but please don't go into management unless you have. If you are a really good operations person then stay out of the strategy arena. I fall into the former category as I am blessed with pragmatism and an ability to see only two colours, black and white. It may not help in visioning workshops but I can get things done.

# VETERANS DAY

**Q:** What is an I.T. Veteran?

**A:** The first thing I've done is to look up a description of veteran in Funk and Wagnall's New Practical Standard Dictionary Volume 2. It was printed in 1956 and given to me a year later by my late father as a 5th birthday present. He did give me Volume 1 as well to preclude a somewhat impressionable child thinking the alphabet only went from M to Z. The description I have picked out describes a veteran as someone who has had experience or practice extending over a long period. This makes me very much a veteran.

In 2000, when I was invited to take on the UK and Ireland operation of a Scandinavian professional services company, I was described in a newspaper article as a veteran and that was over a decade ago. What does that make me now? A question I prefer to leave as rhetorical thank you very much.

I think anybody who spends 40 years in the I.T. business should become a member of a very exclusive veterans club and at the very least be presented with a medal for tenacity and bloody-mindedness if nothing else. In the UK we have Armistice Day. In the USA it's Veterans Day. In 2012, not only will the Olympic Games come to town but I will also celebrate 40 years in I.T. and health permitting, my 60th birthday. This would be a great time to establish the I.T. veterans club as I will meet all the entry criteria, mainly because I've written them.

To gain membership each applicant would have to attend a strenuous assessment centre to ascertain whether they possess the credentials to attain exclusivity. It would be a similar process to what you have to do to become a member of some of the more established and prestigious clubs in London's West End - but much tougher.

In order to be considered for membership, the applicant must be able to provide evidence of 40 years in I.T. and give examples of the following: -

- Via a 15-minute presentation using acetates and not a laptop / projector, describe exactly how they screwed up a very important project and what they learned from the experience.
- How a live incident was resolved purely by shouting at people.

- How one can survive overnight support rosters purely based on takeaways.
- How to become a hero with at least 3 examples of heroic behaviour whilst on paid overtime.
- How to get a bigger office, with nicer carpets and more expensive pictures.
- How to take 3 hours for lunch, especially when your manager thinks you are still in the office.
- How to write a defect-free program using only 16kb of main memory accompanied by a detailed description on how program overlays work.
- How to assess the maturity of an I.T. organisation by smell alone.
- How to legitimately claim unauthorised expenses while abroad on business.
- Why business class travel is the only way to go. Examples of personal exotic holidays taken with subsequent air miles awarded, will add positively to the membership decision.
- How to attend a conference and not attend any of the sessions.
- Explain how the developers of today don't know they're born.

If you can convince me that you have a full grasp of these dozen trials, then you will automatically be granted life membership of the veterans club. If you are unable to step up to the plate on any of them then the question 'What on earth have you been doing all these years?' springs to mind.

## VIEW FROM THE BRIDGE

**Q:** I need a Vision Statement to galvanise our organisation. Have you any bright ideas?

**A:** Always. Don't have a vision statement. Treat it in a similar way that you might a Mission Statement. However I am avoiding a serious question again and probably run the risk of duplicating a previous answer, again!!

What do you want to achieve? Reduced costs, shiny happy people, delighted customers, a smaller system landscape, improved quality, faster development, a smaller support team, higher level of re-use, a reduction in legacy platforms, a reduction in the number of suppliers or contractors? Probably some of these I imagine and maybe even more.

Why not pick out a couple of the most important ones, particularly those that appeal to both customers and employees alike. A Vision Statement along the lines of 'In 3-years time, we will deliver the same amount of working software with half the staff' may be the way to go, but will only satisfy one side of the house.

Another could be 'Reduce the amount of rework caused by quality problems, by 25% over the next 3 years'. This is a laudable goal but not very exciting. It won't catch the imagination. It will not transform anything on its own.

As I've previously stated on more than one occasion, my mission in life is to be a little bit better than crap at what I do. I believe this keeps my feet firmly on the ground and precludes any delusions of grandeur setting in. It has been mentioned to me that I shouldn't use the word crap in a book like this as people won't take it seriously and some may be offended.

In my defence, this is a personal goal and those who are offended need to get out more. I am not suggesting that it is super-imposed on to a banner or poster and splattered all over the office. I should also point out that Funk and Wagnalls 1956 Volume One also describes crapulence as a noun meaning eating or drinking too much and crapulent, an adjective describing drunkenness. I have no idea why but I rest my case on the crap issue.

A vision statement for any initiative is quite a tricky one. It must convey a message of working in a different way and yet not alienate the workforce or make it feel patronised, which is not easy by any stretch of the imagination. Well that's posters out of the equation. I like Better, Cheaper and Faster but that's been used before. I like 'if you don't know where you are any road will do' but that's an old Chinese proverb and I can't just recommend statements willy-nilly just because I like the words. They must have some relevance to the question.

The World War 1 slogan 'Lions led by Donkeys' may cause offence and is probably not where you want your company to go even though it may result in this, if it is not managed properly. 'Sort I.T. out' is good but will probably be treated with derision even though that's what you are doing. Wow – this is difficult!

OK I've got it, a Eureka moment fuelled by my passion for Formula 1 racing and red wine! It's still very cheesy but it's the best I can do!

The statement is 'FIRING ON ALL 6'. You must then describe the six most important things that you want to achieve in your organisation, prioritise them, plan them and then deliver them. That's the best I can do and explains why I leave it to others to pursue careers in marketing.

But I can't leave it there, as that would really be a cop out. So I've looked back at organisations I've worked for in the past and selected half a dozen common themes. I'm afraid there is nothing new here and some of them I have gone on and on and on about in this book although I am convinced that if these are focused on, successfully resourced with good people and then implemented, some magic will happen. It depends on where you are when you start as to the impact. Try firing on all of these:-

1.  Assess your capability in all I.T. disciplines to create a stake in the ground from which to move forward. As a very wise man once said 'If you don't know where you are a map won't help'.
2.  Implement more contemporary development methods that really focus on customer delivery – remember if it's of no use to the customer, then it's of no use to you.
3.  Get rid of defects early – don't expect testing to find them as it won't get them all if you've done nothing about removing them before you get there.
4.  Make sure every project has a plan and it is tracked and reviewed on a regular basis by the team and even senior management. It's not all down to the project manager to do this stuff.

198

5. Automate as much as possible – Re-use as much as possible.
6. Get your estimating right. Focus on predictability not perfection! Make sure everyone learns.

## VISUAL INSANITY

**Q:** We have a number of meeting rooms equipped with state of the art video conferencing facilities. The meeting rooms are always fully booked but rarely does any video conferencing take place. What a complete waste of money. Is it me?

**A:** Of all the questions that you could have asked me in the 'V' category, you have chosen this one. What about all the victorious projects where victory was stolen from the jaws of defeat? Or is it the other way round? I'm never too sure.

One of the problems I personally have with video conferencing is that it looks quite complicated to set up and I'm never sure what button to press to make it work. If it was around 20 or 30 years ago there would have been someone in a long light brown coat that would come in and set it all up in advance. Sadly the days of the brown coat have passed and with them the end of an era.

I also find that many people who work in I.T. are the worst when it comes to exploiting technology. We are all very virtuous and sanctimonious when it comes to telling other people to use technology more, but some of us are completely useless ourselves.

Perhaps one way of getting people to use it more often would be to charge the meeting attendees for hiring the room unless video conferencing was used. It seems a bit petty though and would invoke the expensive services of an overhead support group to monitor it.

Ironically, human nature leads us to prefer face-to-face meetings, which is particularly strange as communication sessions rarely happen in a face-to-face way.

Face-to-Face is all very well if the attendees are in the same town or city but a trifle expensive if you are in another city, country, continent or time zone. So we need to use the technology. What hope do we have in getting an organisation to use a new tool in a consistent fashion when we can't switch on a TV and phone?

As a humorous aside, and goodness knows this answer needs an injection of humour, I remember a meeting I attended when we agreed to experiment with video conferencing. There were 3 separate locations involved, two of which were in the same city. 2 out of 3 locations successfully engaged, even though the picture had a mind of its own. The 3$^{rd}$ location dialled in on audio and they were in the same city as the group that used video conferencing. They couldn't even be bothered to travel 2 miles from one side of the city to the other. What chance do we have? These people are the same ones who go home in the evening and compliment the family on their use of web-cams to speak to friends and family.

If all else fails I suggest management communicate a policy that travel expenses will not be reimbursed when video conferencing facilities are available. Hell hath no fury like anyone who hasn't had his or her expenses paid.

Other questions that you could have asked me starting with 'V': -

1.  Why do people get so excited about the V-model for testing?

2.  What is Virtual I/O?

3.  What is the penalty in Bridge when you go 2 under and are Vulnerable?

4.  Have you been to Venice?

5.  Do agile methods encourage vague requirements?

6.  Did you get my Voice-Mail (LOL)?

*'People who **Work** sitting down get paid more than people who work standing up' – Ogden Nash*

**WAR IN THE WORKPLACE**

**Q:** Do you have an I.T. veteran's war story that you can share?

**A:** I trust that you are not squeamish but what I am about to describe did take place, well most of it did. It was the worst time of my career and not something I look back on with any pride at all. Where do I start? Firstly with an apology because I should have walked away from this project at the beginning as it was simply not doable. My heart said it was but my head said otherwise. Sadly I regret carrying on, as I didn't have the courage to risk my career for something I believed. In the end, business circumstances and politics caused the project to be canned and I left the company anyway. It was a very dark part of my career and I backed many lame horses.

This was to be one of the largest projects this particular company had ever undertaken. Alarm bells were ringing but I was not listening. In years to come I was to discover that there is no record of anything of this size being implemented successfully. What I really should have tried to do was get the scope reduced, while many around me were increasing it, in the misguided belief that large is good and points make prizes.

The new system was to be taken on by the whole company and not just the retail arm so we had a very large group of seriously senior executives who had no interest in what we were being asked to do. It was being forced fed to them and certainly not something they could buy in to. However, the commandment from on high was that the Board had agreed that one solution will fit all so get on with it! It was madness to expect the I.T. people to be the only ones pushing this 'global' message, as we were always going to be the meat in a very large club sandwich. I also don't think we believed it was possible either.

So, with all this political mumbo-jumbo going on in the background and with only one or two members of the I.T. executive board supporting what we were trying to do, we launched the project. We were armed with a high-level scope document that was actually good enough to go with, but for some strange reason we all agreed that it would be a great idea to go down to a much more detailed level with the requirements. We then spent the next year documenting these low level requirements and asking for them to be signed-off by about 20 different people, all with their own political axe to grind. This took forever, wasted so much time but in the end we had a signed-off set of requirements albeit with the caveats being larger in volume than the actual requirements themselves. If awards were given out to projects based on the weight of their requirements then anybody would have struggled to match us. We would be world champions, even with double-sided printing.

In parallel to this (this war story uses this phrase a lot), all of the development effort was now to take place using a new tool that nobody had ever heard of. Now, call me old-fashioned, but I now had a floor full of people who had gone home on a Friday night really understanding how to do development in the existing environment and were now sitting in front of a new tool on Monday morning, without any clue as to what button to press to make the damned thing work. Not only that, we had no quality support from the supplier, no standards, no templates and no training plans in place – zilch! How were my people going to learn not only how to work with the tool but the different approaches to development that were mandatory to exploit the iterative opportunities it offered?

To get all this done, and it was done, put us back another year. It seemed like everybody in the company was putting every possible obstacle in front of us and the only people who thought the tool was a great idea, were those who had no responsibility whatsoever for making it work and certainly had no intention whatsoever of using it on their projects. The management were, shall we say, already distancing themselves from both the project and this wretched tool.

In parallel to this, the organisation was in the process of introducing a new resource management system where feedback was encouraged in order to get those helicopter and holistic 360-degree views of an individual's performance. Fantastic! So instead of walking the floor and seeing prototypes of the emerging transactions on my teams' desktops, all I could see was literally a sea of employee feedback forms. I did my best to overturn this nonsense by screaming at the people responsible but was simply told I was being negative. At the end of the first month of this initiative, I had also received around 50 requests for feedback, some from people who I'd only met once or twice in the lift on the way up to my desk. What on earth was I supposed to feedback? I asked Joe for the 3$^{rd}$ floor and he pressed the button numbered 3 with absolute perfection.

In parallel to this, we launched a software process improvement initiative based on the Capability Maturity Model for Software (a trademark of the Software Engineering Institute). This was carefully couched in such a way that if the new processes couldn't be deployed on my project then they wouldn't work anywhere else. Now don't get me wrong, I am a great believer in processes that when used, result in the best outcome for the customer. I wasn't always this view but I am now. So I embraced the initiative and tried my best to make it happen. Sadly though, it turned out to be just a welcome distraction from the job in hand, as opposed to something nuclear that would really make the project take off. It even got to the stage where the process became more important than the project and it was the biggest mistake I have ever made. I carried those scars around with me for a number of years until some level of pragmatism and self-esteem returned. I let many people down, including myself.

In parallel to this, we had a Change Council but to be fair this didn't distract us that much because it was fairly obvious that senior management didn't really want to change anything and if they did they may well have chosen a different set of people to make it happen, with a couple of notable exceptions.

In parallel to this, the emerging migration strategy to lead us from the harsh reality of legacy systems to the brave new world was taking shape. I still maintain to this day that it was fundamentally flawed because it took absolutely no account of my development challenges. It relied on all software being ready irrespective of where it was in the development cycle. This put even more pressure on delivery and instead of 'bending' the strategy to make it work for me, we retained a strategy that was logical, pure, well thought through, independently produced but totally unrealistic. There was also no appetite for revisiting it with the senior executive sponsors and to this day I do not understand why.

In parallel to this, we were going to implement on brand new hardware platforms. I can't comment too much on this as it really didn't impact me that much but seemed to add to an already increasing risk burden. I was losing the will to live and not doing the best job I possibly could. Everywhere I went seemed to self-destruct by the time I got my hands on it.

There were a lot of other new initiatives kicking off during this period but again they can't have had a major impact on me because the sands of time have erased the details. However, I started to formulate my escape plan as more and more people questioned the implementability of what we were striving so hard to achieve.

In the end I lasted 4 years, others stayed longer but as you can imagine, our failure to deliver destroyed the original business case and it flew out of the window. The final kiss of death was a merger where new management came in and took an instant dislike to the colour of our tin and the project was cancelled. By this time, I was long gone and earning the king's shilling as a mercenary elsewhere but it took a number of years before I recovered my confidence and was able to really do some great work again. It was a war and a true learning experience. Again, you just had to be there.

War teaches you things. It teaches you that you are only as good as your last battle. It teaches you not to trust everybody. It teaches you that small is good and getting software built and tested quickly is far better than a rain forest of documentation that nobody really wanted and certainly nobody really cared about or read. It teaches you never to go into battle on too many fronts. It teaches you that great processes can never be an excuse for not producing a great solution for your customers. It teaches you that it is impossible to predict the impact of a merger. It teaches you that yesterday's enemy could become your line manager of tomorrow, and he did!

Although these were the Dark Ages of my career, like in any war, there was the odd ceasefire and trip abroad to provide some short-term light relief. One of the nicest trips I had was to a reference site that used the tool we were striving to implement. I stayed in a hotel that had one of the top 5 bars in the world.

The business end of the visit was a total waste of time and money as I was given no opportunity to ask any technical questions but the beer was absolutely exquisite. It wasn't all bad!

## WHISKY AND WILD WILD SCHEDULES

**Q:** What is the whisky syndrome?

**A:** Is this where you dreamt that a massive project was successfully delivered only to wake up and realise it was only a whisky-fuelled dream?

I find that whisky and project schedules aren't a great combination. You end up with an over-optimistic plan that can't be delivered and a stinking headache for your troubles. At least if your manager asks if you were drunk when you put the plan together, you can at least answer - 'Probably!'

This is what is known in the trade as padding. I'm pretty confident you have mis-spelt whisky and maybe referring to the W.I.S.C.Y syndrome. This goes back a long way and was particularly prevalent when there was an explosion of 'blokeware' being developed by apparently intelligent non-I.T. people over a weekend. Why do I need to wait for I.T. to do this when I can knock up a quick spreadsheet on a Sunday afternoon?

W.I.S.C.Y probably means 'Why Isn't Someone Coding Yet?' It's ironic that many people, including myself, used to be somewhat sharp with people who asked this question a few days after the requirements had been agreed. 'Don't be ridiculous' we'd cry as we have a lot of analysis and design to do and a shed-load of documentation to produce before we can even consider coding.

How times have changed! Yes the people who used to ask the W.I.S.C.Y question at that time were ill-informed peasants. This is especially true of people whose idea of detailed requirements was 'Do Lots of Banking Stuff Now' and if we couldn't fulfil this ridiculous request then I.T. were not stepping up to the plate in their eyes.

Nowadays there is a refreshing move towards methods that encourage you to get into the coding phase as early as humanly possible and I may well be one of those people asking the W.I.S.C.Y question. There is a lot of merit in producing something that customers can touch and feel as soon as possible. It precludes analysis paralysis but does need the business and I.T. teams to work closely and both wanting to achieve the same goals. You can't have the situation where the scope of a release is frozen too early and is then subject to rigid change control that squeezes the breath and will to live out of the customer. Alternatively, you can't have the situation where something is added to the contents of a release but scope of equivalent value is not removed to accommodate it.

So welcome, albeit kicking and struggling, to the exclusive world of W.I.S.C.Y. I joined a couple of years ago and nothing has happened since to make me cancel my membership.

## WARRANTY WORRIES ME

**Q:** Why is there such a flurry of activity in the warranty period immediately following a live implementation? I have just completed an analysis of the huge number of hours booked to warranty activities. The results are quite extraordinary.

**A:** This is a complete nonsense. This behaviour plays havoc with schedules, budgets and portfolios alike. I simply do not understand the concept of keeping the development team together for a period after a release goes live purely on the basis that something might go horribly wrong. It doesn't speak very highly of the effectiveness of work done by the development and testing teams in terms of quality or handover.

I have even seen change requests raised and approved for inclusion within the warranty period. This is not good, not good at all. It's almost as if everybody is scared of releasing the resources in case anything goes wrong. This is bad enough when a project is delivered to schedule but this isn't usually the case. Resources are retained longer than planned and new projects are then delayed or are initiated inefficiently, as the required resources are still sitting around waiting for a previous project to finish or go wrong or even worse, are working on newly identified features from un-prioritised change requests.

I think warranties should be eliminated as a concept. If the support and test teams are engaged at the right time, then surely they are the best placed to do any warranty work given they will have ongoing responsibility for the support of the solution. Obviously you wouldn't expose them and continued access to the development team is vital for consultancy and clarification but not 100% of the time.

I suspect it is fear of the unknown that drives this behaviour coupled with inadequate engagement before and during test. The best solution is for warranties to form part of the project budget but only plan for support and test people to recover their costs from it, with a much smaller amount estimated for consumption by the development team, who should be working on the next set of requirements for a different project.

# WASTE MANAGEMENT

**Q:** How can I reduce the amount of wasted effort that my people perform on non-chargeable activities?

**A:** How do you know it's wasted effort and can't be charged to a project? It's a serious question. It is often assumed that project management is an overhead and therefore cannot be charged to a project. This, by the way, is complete nonsense and should only be challenged if the project management effort exceeds 20% of the overall budget or maybe less than 15%, as this may not be enough. Some projects where everything is well understood may not require a project manager, but there still needs to be project management.

It varies greatly across the organisational spectrum as to which activities are chargeable and which are non-chargeable. It is obviously in everyone's interest if the effort can be capitalised and the cost spread over a longer period, rather than an immediate hit on the profit and loss account. There are strict rules around this so consult your local bean counter if unsure.

So wasted and non-chargeable aren't necessarily the same thing. All waste should be kept to an absolute minimum. Some waste is necessary and inevitable but ensure that what looks like waste today, will become fruitful tomorrow.

It is difficult to allocate the costs of improvements to a single project so this may simply have to be taken on the chin and booked as non-chargeable work unless a business sponsor can be found. As managers it is our responsibility to track all costs and benefits on a regular basis. We must ensure that our customers are getting value for money. If a small unit is set up to address quality issues then make sure it stays small. These groups have a habit of snowballing into large teams of people to provide some sort of justification of the manager's job title and remuneration package.

The easiest way to contain non-chargeable activities is to restrict the availability of finance codes against which people can recover their time. It shocks me that so many people are surprised by the amount of time taken up on non-project work and it often needs an expensive efficiency study or assessment to highlight these issues.

The life blood of any I.T. organisation is its projects and they need to be delivered as efficiently as possible. Why not take a triage approach to non-chargeable activities. If the patient will survive without non-chargeable treatment then don't do anything. If the patient is going to die anyway, irrespective of non-chargeable treatment, then don't do anything either. Focus all your efforts on activities where some form of treatment will add value to the assets and the patient will definitely survive and flourish as a result. This will keep overheads at an acceptable level.

Haven't we been here before?

# X

*'We're just making plans for Nigel' - XTC*

**I WONDERED WHERE I COULD FIT XYLOPHONE IN!**

**Q:** If I.T. had an X-Factor competition, what sort of person would win it?

**A:** A very special leader - someone that can display all of the following characteristics, one for each letter of the alphabet.

**A**ssertive – always lets you know what is wanted and why.
**B**rave – never shirks from making the difficult call.
**C**harismatic – makes people sit up and listen.
**D**etermined – always delivers on promises.
**E**nergetic – puts everything into the job.
**F**air – always treats people with respect.
**G**alvanising – gets everyone to step up to the plate.
**H**onest – people always believe what they're being told.
**I**ntuitive – doesn't always go for the easiest option.
**J**ust – people always get a fair crack of the whip.
**K**nowledgeable – people come for advice and guidance.
**L**ogical – thinks through every decision to make sure it makes sense.
**M**entor – happy to share experience and guide people along the right path.
**N**urturing – keen to grow a learning organisation.
**O**pen – door is often open and mouth is often shut.
**P**ragmatic – feet firmly on the ground.
**Q**uestioning – challenges people to deliver great things.
**R**ealistic – doesn't commit to ridiculous deadlines and solutions.
**S**trategic – plans ahead - makes things happen instead of wondering what happened.
**T**hought provoking – makes people think about what they're doing.
**U**nstinting – gives praise when due and also the opposite when it isn't.
**V**isionary – can see the big picture.
**W**ise – uses own experiences in decision-making.
**X**-Factor – certainly has it if all the other 25 characteristics are in place.

**Y**outhful – is contemporary in outlook, if not in years.

**Z**ealous – is passionate about everyone in the company doing a fantastic job.

If this reminds you of you, then I'd really like to meet up because so far in my career, you have been conspicuous by your absence.

For those readers who have no idea what the X-Factor is, it is a singing competition that is omnipresent on various UK channels and the winner gets a major recording contract that usually but not always results in a Christmas Number One hit record. It is unlikely that the winner will possess all of the above characteristics as they are usually young people and a little bit me, me, me!

# XXX

Never let it be said that this author failed to rise to the challenge of addressing the X problem. I can't answer any more questions as I only ever received one and I've just had a stab at it. What I can do is offer some observations where X appears somewhere but not always where you might expect it.

**Q:** What do you think of Xtreme programming?

**A:** See what I've done there – a very intuitive use of the letter X. It would be somewhat hypocritical of me to answer it, given my view that unless you have jumped into a swimming pool on horseback, you can't really write a book on water polo. I have only read books on Xtreme programming, is what I'm trying to say, in my usual analogous fashion.

However, I do have a lot of time for any approach to software development that focuses on getting to the build stage as quickly as possible and delivering real value early. Carry on chaps!

**Q:** Why do we need to X-reference requirements?

**A:** If you don't, then how do you know whether they have been designed and built into the solution? How can you perform full coverage on testing? I would not only cross-reference requirements but also size them, value them and prioritise them, in case some need to be deferred until the next release or forever. Yawn!

**Q:** My project is turning into an X-Rated horror movie. Have you worked on any of these and what's the best way of avoiding the vampires?

**A:** I most certainly have and have nearly seen blood on the streets. I'm not sure that I.T. people can solve this particular problem on their own. Most projects that go bad in my experience are because the scope is too large and the teams often have no data with which to accurately size the effort in order to produce quality estimates. The business case is therefore only built on sand.

Industry data that is generally available shows quite clearly that when a project is over a certain size, it fails to meet its goals. It may still deliver, but only when it's ready. It is a quest as opposed to something that can be planned, executed and delivered with any confidence whatsoever.

Small is the way to go but how small? I've no idea but the most effective projects I've worked on have been with small teams of around 5 or 6 people, delivering functionality of 1,000 function points or less in an elapsed time of 3-6 months.

**Q:** I.T. people enjoy a good party. What's your favourite Xmas party story and before you answer this, again please bear in mind children may be reading this?

**A:** I've never been a big fan of office parties as there's so much expectation and little opportunity for impromptu activities. I think the best ones are those that don't start off as a party but evolve into one. Nevertheless you have asked a decent, if off-topic question, and it deserves a decent family-friendly answer.

This is the amazing tale of the Flying Sambuca Brothers, who were neither brothers nor could they fly but I believe there is no need to let the whole truth get in the way of a good story.

On this particular year, the office bash was arranged to start in the afternoon but I had another business commitment, so I couldn't get there until early in the evening. Don't you just love it when you get to a party and everyone else has been drinking for 4-5 hours? The tables were in the death throes of being cleared up after 40 or so meals had been devoured by what looked like a pack of animals.

Liqueurs were in the process of being served and let me assure you that this particular congregation needed a liqueur like I need a third nostril. Three of the guys had furtively ensconced themselves at a smaller table that had obviously been unused throughout the afternoon's war games, given its pristine status.

This gleesome threesome had decided that now was the time to order Flaming Sambucas. For the sensible ones amongst you, I should explain that Sambuca is a clear drink flavoured with anise that can be served hot with 2 or 3 flaming coffee beans. Apparently, this adds to the 'experience' and explains why the drink is so named.

The Flaming Sambucas arrived and standard procedure is to extinguish the flames, let the glass cool down a touch and then down the warm liquid in one slug. This can go one of two ways. It is either an exciting bodily experience or something you will never ever do again as long as you live. This trio however introduced an innovation that I hadn't seen performed live up until then.

They attempted to down the Flaming Sambucas without extinguishing the fiery liquid. I'm not sure if all three mental giants spat out the flaming liquid but enough heat was despatched on to the paper tablecloth to ignite it. Fortunately, an alert waiter cleverly extinguished the fire by pouring the contents of a full water jug on to both the flames and the three pyromaniacs. However this was not before they had tried to put the flames out themselves by throwing Amoretti papers at them. Yes, when you are in a state of sobriety, you know that Amoretti biscuits are wrapped in very thin flammable paper and wouldn't dream of doing something that equates to trying to extinguish a fire with petrol.

So our Three Musketeers retired to the bathroom to clean up, dry off and maybe have one more shot at the title. However, I believe they must have seen the waiter's expression and thought the better of it. Around 15 minutes later, our trio returned to the fray all sporting slightly damp trousers and identical burn marks at the corners of their mouths. Explain that when you get home!

I guess you had to be there!


**Q:** Have you ever thought of taking up the Xylophone?

**A:** Stop it!

# Y

*'Do or Do Not...there is no try' – **Yoda***

## ALL OF OUR YESTERDAYS

**Q:** It is quite obvious that in my organisation we have a ridiculous number of projects kicking off at the same time. We have a finite number of people to work on projects, as the vast majority are either putting out live support fires or in an overhead role. Has it always been like this or was it different in your day?

**A:** In my day indeed!! So the secret is out. I am a man with his career all behind him. The answer to your question is probably. The big difference is that in my day as you refer to it, only a handful of people knew of the existence of a portfolio of projects, they worked in the I.T. department and so really understood what was realistic and achievable. They could also throttle back on the amount of work in progress to preclude any logjams. Of course there were Red or struggling projects but these were an exception and rarely reported on. It's only in recent years that I've seen so many organisations in trouble due to their failure to start projects properly. Just because there is 200 man-years worth of budget available for new projects, it really doesn't all have to be spent by the end of the first quarter.

It seems pretty commonplace that many projects are launched as Green for Go when they should at the very least be Amber for proceed with caution or Red for Stop. It is never a popular move to have a non-Green project early in its development but if you haven't got what you need then what's the point in continuing. At the very least you must take some short, sharp, time-bound actions to keep the project on track, so it has some chance of success.

I'm not sure why Green projects are not challenged more. This will avoid the scenario where a 20-week project has 18 weeks of Green, 1 week of Red

216

and then moves to a brownish colour from which there is little chance of recovery.

Although this is a short chapter, it would be remiss of me, as a person who has lived most of his life within 50 miles of London, not to have a good old sing-along to finish. I hope litigation will not ensue.

The song is based on the Beatles classic - Yesterday. The lyrics have changed somewhat but you can sing the same tune if you so wish – seems to work.

YESTERDAY ALL MY PROJECTS WERE GREEN I'D SAY
NOW IT LOOKS AS IF THEY'RE NOT OKAY
I DON'T BELIEVE IN YESTERDAY

SUDDENLY, THERE IS HALF THE SCOPE THERE USED TO BE
THE BUSINESS CASE HAS BEEN DUMPED AT SEA
AND REDS CREPT UP SO SUDDENLY

WHY THERE WERE NO PLANS
I DON'T KNOW, I COULDN'T SAY
NOW THERE'S SO MUCH WRONG
HOW I LONG FOR YESTERDAY

YESTERDAY I.T. WAS SUCH AN EASY GAME TO PLAY
NOW THERE'S NO PLACE TO HIDE AWAY
SO SIZE 10 BOOTS WILL COME MY WAY

WHY I HAVE NO JOB
IT'S NOT FAIR, I'M NOT TO BLAME
I'VE DONE NOTHING WRONG
HOW I LONG FOR SEVERANCE PAY

YESTERDAY ALL MY PROJECTS WERE NOT GREEN OK
THEY WERE RED I SHOULD HAVE HAD MY SAY
I DON'T BELIEVE IN YESTERDAY

Thunderous applause – and exit stage left and pronto.

217

# Z

*'To know what you know and what you do not know, that is true knowledge'*
*– Kong Fu **Zi***

## ZODIAC OF I.T. – THE HORROR SCOPES

As I complete my epic journey through the alphabet, I thought I'd finish with a bit of panache and some style with an I.T. slant to the 13, yes 13 signs of the I.T. Zodiac. Each star sign is described in a way that depicts both strengths and weaknesses of the individual born under its influence, accompanied by a not so subtle suggestion about the type of I.T. role that may best suit these people. Other interesting habits are also included along with some additional information for the purists. Enjoy but don't read on if you are easily offended!

### ARIES THE RAM - March 20th to April 19th
You are very adventurous with an honest and loyal disposition. Independence is very important to you and you possess a strong intellect. Unfortunately, this is countered by an impatient, sometimes foolhardy nature and you flare up very quickly. You act on impulse and never let data get in the way of a good guess. You are very dynamic, in as much as you rant at your I.T. people at every opportunity and are usually given a wide berth when estimates are ready for review. You do make an ideal user.
**Additional information:** You are a Fire sign, have a penchant for Cayenne Pepper and Birmingham is a favourite UK city. Your favourite colour is RED which explains a lot.

### TAURUS THE BULL – April 20th to May 20th
You are a patient and reliable soul who hides a determined and persistent attitude very well. Your colleagues have no idea that you have a bushel to hide anything under. On the down side you can be jealous, possessive and resentful and someone who will only work on specific tasks that were spelt out in blood at your interview and etched in stone on your employment

218

contract. You border on the greedy and talk massive amounts of bull that is so consistent with your star sign. Ever tried consulting?

**Additional information**: You are an Earth sign, your favourite colour is Pink and you are partial to Cloves, Sorrel and Spearmint.

## GEMINI THE TWINS – May 21<sup>st</sup> to June 20<sup>th</sup>

You are without doubt a great communicator who is both eloquent and witty. Indeed thou art a very bright spark indeed. Versatility and adaptability are the names of your game and you belong in an agile world of cunning and inconsistency. You can be tense and nervous especially around waterfall lifecycles and your inquisitive nature borders on the nosy. As a twin you extol the virtues of paired programming and make a first-class master of agility and all things lean.

**Additional information:** You are an Air sign and, although most colours appeal, Yellow is a particular favourite. You thoroughly enjoy the fruit of nut bearing trees and love to travel the world, in particular Plymouth, Cardiff and San Francisco.

## CANCER THE CRAB – June 21<sup>st</sup> to July 22<sup>nd</sup>

You are emotional, loving and protective of your colleagues, especially in times of crises such as soggy lettuce in the company canteen salad or a cold coffee from the dispensing machine. You are a shrewd beast proceeding cautiously across a stretch of office like a crab conducting a pincer movement. To your detriment, you are partial to the occasional mood swing and tend to cling on to past successes as if they will in some way save your future bacon. You have a tendency to overreact emotionally and can appear touchy, particularly when the nasty I.T. director wants to know what the hell's going on. Team Leader material if ever I saw it.

**Additional information:** You are a Water sign with a love of all things Silver Grey in colour. You enjoy the company of creatures with a shell covering and love eating vegetables with high water content.

## LEO THE LION – July 23<sup>rd</sup> to August 22<sup>nd</sup>

You have roar energy. Your strengths are definitely your generosity in the bar, your creative juices and your strict adherence to never paying overtime. You are faithful to causes, especially lost ones and your pompous and often patronising interference when there is a live problem stands you in good stead to become an executive legend. Mix these ingredients with a scintilla of intolerance and a soupcon of bossiness and the Porsche will be on order before you can say 'Where's my next promotion coming from?' Hello Senior Executive! Jump into your box of goodies.

219

**Additional information:** You are a Fire sign ruled by the Sun. You love Sunflowers and Marigolds along with Ruby Gemstones. Wanderlust often takes you to Rome, Prague, Bombay, Madrid, Philadelphia, Chicago, Los Angeles, Bath and Bristol.

## VIRGO THE VIRGIN – August 23$^{rd}$ to September 22$^{nd}$
Your modesty and innate shyness hide a practical and analytical mind. You are hard working and the most reliable person in the company. Mix this with a reasonable level of intelligence and you may wish to question what on earth you did to deserve a career in I.T. However on the downside you worry for England and come across as a fussy perfectionist. On the Red, Amber and Green spectrum your colour is Forever Red even when it's not. Harsh words maybe but a testing maestro is what you are.
**Additional information:** You are an Earth sign and share a love of all nut-bearing trees with Gemini. You also enjoy any vegetable grown under the earth and your favourite metals are Mercury and Nickel.

## LIBRA THE SCALES – September 23$^{rd}$ to October 22$^{nd}$
You are a charming person who openly displays an easy-going nature. Your diplomatic skills enable you to negotiate the release of political prisoners, if required, and not just the release of software - you old romantic you! Some drawbacks include your blind spot of flirting with the opposition, sorry I meant the customer, and an indecisive self-indulgence. Intertwine this with breathtaking gullibility and the true Customer Relationship Manager tips the scales at 15 gushes per minute.
**Additional information:** You are an Air sign ruled by Venus. You like Ash and Poplar trees with your favourite colours being all shades of Blue up to and including Aquamarine. Travel takes you to Austria, Burma, Japan, Argentina, Upper Egypt and Canada.

## SCORPIO THE SCORPION – October 23$^{rd}$ to November 21$^{st}$
You are a determined and powerful character with a definite sting in your tail. You are prone to emotional outbursts that at times undermine your intuition and ability to smell bull from a different time zone. Your obvious passion for your job, and I mean your job and nobody else's, gives away your jealous and possessive nature. If you finish off this particular recipe with an ounce of obstinacy and a litre of secrecy then you have the role model Middle Management blotting paper.
**Additional information:** You are a Water sign ruled by Pluto. Dark Reds and Maroons are plentiful in your life and you enjoy Crustaceans and most

Insects. A City break will take in New Orleans, Fez, Milwaukee, Liverpool, Halifax or Hull. Watch out for those thick bushy trees.

## SAGITTARIUS THE ARCHER - November 22$^{nd}$ to December 21$^{st}$

You are a freedom-loving, honest and straightforward individual who believes that any problem can be solved on the train journey home. Your sense of humour is legendary and you are equally at ease with the philosophers of the world. Your intellectual capacity and thirst for knowledge reveal a quintessentially blind optimism bundled with a careless, sometimes irresponsible attitude. Your pragmatism is world-class as is your ability to say exactly what you think, irrespective of the damage it may cause and your tendency to be easily bored means you are often an absolute bloody nuisance in meetings. However, because of this potent cocktail of traits, you are the libero, the queller of revolutions and the rebel without a clue. You can be anything and everything. 'A great sign to be born under', notes the author, who just happens to have been born under it.

**Additional information:** You are a Fire sign ruled by Jupiter and, like Mary Poppins, are practically perfect in every way.

## CAPRICORN THE GOAT - December 22$^{nd}$ to January 19$^{th}$

You are patient, diligent and careful with an almost anal tendency to dot every tea and cross every eye. You are very practical with an unhealthy lust for figures and reports. You hate spending any money at all, least of all your own and your pessimistic nature reveals a tendency to be over conventional. You are the archetypal process extremist. Be careful as you are now entering the wonderful world of the bean counter – only kidding!

**Additional information:** You are an Earth sign ruled by Saturn. Flowers play a big part in your life particularly Ivy, Hemlock, Medlar and Heartsease. You enjoy visiting capital cities but only the administrative areas. Until now you have been blissfully unaware that Goat's Cheese smells of Goats.

## AQUARIUS THE WATER BEARER - January 20$^{th}$ to February 18$^{th}$

You have trouble passing water or certainly feel a little dizzy when walking over bridges. Apart from being liquidly challenged, you are friendly, outgoing, honest and loyal. Your independent streak means that you spend a lot of time alone and when not on your own, you love to be surrounded by intellectuals and time wasters. You can be viewed as not only detached and aloof but also perverse and unconventional. Your hippy-like trances can lead others to think you have stopped breathing but a make-up mirror beneath the nostrils reveals that you have simply transcended to the cloud upon which you live. You are free from the manacles of pragmatism and do not possess an operational concern of any kind. This is the Never Never Land of Strategy.

**Additional information:** You are an Air sign and not entirely surprisingly ruled by Uranus. Aluminium plays a massive part in your life and you adore large birds with long flight ability. You insist on all your food being frozen and Turquoise is a favourite colour.

### PISCES THE FISH February 19<sup>th</sup> to March 19<sup>th</sup>

You display a sensitive and compassionate side and always lend a sympathetic ear to the whingers, but only in the company's time. Your kind nature hides a secretive and vague individual who displays cherished competencies, like being easily-led and weak-willed. You are an idealist, who is only happy when all the requirements for a project have been documented to death and signed-off in user-blood even though you know they will in no way influence the finished article. Your analytical mind and ability to elicit outrageously ambiguous diatribes from your customer base puts you in the unenviable position of living in the world of Analysis Paralysis.

**Additional information:** You are a Water sign whose favourite colour is soft Sea-Green. You like trees that grow near water and you like all your mammals to like water too. You adore desserts and your favourite cities include Jerusalem, Santiago di Compostella and Bournemouth.

### ALPHA PROJECTI MANAGERIUS - 1<sup>st</sup> January – 31<sup>st</sup> December

You are very unlucky as you are completely under the influence of the 13<sup>th</sup> sign that not many people know about. You were not born under any sign of the Zodiac. In fact you were not born at all, preferring to be quarried from rocks. If you are a great project manager, then you are indeed a rare breed and if you are not then don't worry as you belong to a club with a huge membership. Great project managers should always be on display in a reception area alongside the other virtually extinct species, the satisfied customer. You are a tenacious character who has an almost unquenchable desire to stare defeat in the face and grasp victory from its snapping jaws at the eleventh hour or certainly 23 hours 59 minutes into Go Live Day -1.

You have a real skill for not being informed about every decision made on your project and an almost rabid focus on an out of date and irrelevant Risk Log. You are continually amazed that your Project Management Practitioner certificate, although looking very much at home in your office, does not actually make you a better Project Manager. You are a healthy cynic who passionately believes that tomorrow will always be better than today, purely on the basis that it can't be any worse, and you believe winter lasts all year as it is always dark when you leave the house in the morning and also when you return at night. Your bonus is awarded mainly out of sympathy and although you desire a sports car, you will never own one based on your project manager's salary alone. You deserve better!

**Additional information:** You were born under a very tired sign and your favourite colour is Green, although you own few things of this colour. You hate all things Red, get particularly nervous around anything Amber and your dream is to finish something – anything!

## AND ZEN – THE FINALE

And finally, with the author now foaming at the mouth, a troubled and tortured soul, he asks himself - 'What is the point of all this nonsense? Has it been worth it? Is there an I.T. God and if so why has he deserted me?' I have repeated myself on many of my hot buttons in the dim and distant hope that one of them might stick. I make no apology for this.

After careful consideration, I propose two answers to the unasked question about my vision, following my I.T. adventures. The first is based on my current state of mind, the other on my desired state. The reader can conclude which one is the best place for me to be.

**VISION 1:** I still just want to be a little bit better than crap.

**VISION 2:** This is much deeper and more profound. I first heard this at a company conference I attended over 20 years ago. I was pretty cheesed off at the time as the conference was held on a Saturday and my team were playing at home. The following quote is the only thing I remember from that complete and utter waste of time and money, so it must have made quite an impression on me. It has stood the test of time and is attributed to an unnamed Zen Buddhist and here it is:-

*'The Master in the art of living makes little distinction between his work and his play, his labour and his leisure, his mind and his body, his education and his recreation, his love and his religion. He simply pursues his vision of excellence in whatever he does, leaving others to decide whether he is working or playing. To him, he is always doing both'.*

# EPILOGUE

Well thanks for sticking with it. It's difficult to comprehend how I managed to take over five years to complete this book. I guess it's an indication of the fast pace of change in the I.T. sector and confirmation that every single day is different and you learn something new every day as well. I am also a lazy sod!

I am happy to admit there is a fair amount of duplication in the book and the reason for this is quite simple. Many questions and issues have the same answer. Many answers have to be repeated to get the message across.

I will leave you with five major conclusions from lessons I have learnt, wars that I have fought and battles that I have won and lost. My scars and wounds have healed but the journey continues. For that, I am eternally grateful.

1.  True success is only achievable if you have a total focus on delighting your customers and your people.

2.  I.T. people are at their most productive when they operate in self-organising teams, in an environment free of fear and blame. Command and control needs to be buried at sea.

3.  Customers are happier when their suppliers deliver quality products in short, sharp iterations of features that add considerable value to their business.

4.  Trust, empowerment and feeling valued mean more than anything to your people.

5.  Never accept the status quo – challenge everything – improve continuously – have fun – make great things happen!

**Wow – is that it? Guess so – Bye then!**

www.ingramcontent.com/pod-product-compliance
Lightning Source LLC
Chambersburg PA
CBHW051452170526
45166CB00001B/213